# CELEBRATING
# BIRCH

## THE LORE, ART, AND CRAFT OF AN ANCIENT TREE

# CELEBRATING
# BIRCH

### THE LORE, ART, AND CRAFT OF AN ANCIENT TREE

BY NORTH HOUSE FOLK SCHOOL

FOX CHAPEL
PUBLISHING

*Cover Photography*
PHILIP BOWEN
LAYNE KENNEDY
DEBORAH SUSSEX

*Step-by-Step Photography*
PHILIP BOWEN

*Editorial Photography*
LAYNE KENNEDY

*Gallery Photography*
DEBORAH SUSSEX

*Contributing Photographers*
RICK BROOKER
JAY STEINKE
NORTH HOUSE FOLK SCHOOL

*Illustration*
BETSY BOWEN

*Design, Editorial, and Manuscript*
BETSY BOWEN
SCOTT POLLOCK
ANNE PRINSEN
HARLEY REFSAL
GREG WRIGHT
JOHN ZASADA

*Celebrating Birch* is an original work, first published in 2007 by Fox Chapel Publishing Company, Inc.
The photographs and illustrations that appear in this book are copyrighted by the individual
photographers and artists. "Language," by Joanne Hart, copyright 1992, was previously published in *Witch
Tree: A Collaboration*, with Hazel Belvo, Holy Cow! Press, Duluth, MN. Reprinted with permission.

ISBN 978-1-56523-307-2

Publisher's Cataloging-in-Publication Data
     Celebrating birch : the lore, art and craft of an ancient
     tree / by the North House Folk School. -- East
     Petersburg, PA : Fox Chapel Publishing, c2007.

         p. ; cm.

         Summary: Includes a broad history of the birch tree,
     plus 20 practical woodworking projects to create.
         ISBN-13: 978-1-56523-307-2

         1. Wood-carving. 2. Woodwork. 3. Birch--Folklore.
     4. Birch--Utilization. 5. Folk art--Patterns. I. North House
     Folk School. II. Title: Lore, art and craft of an ancient
     tree.
                        0708

TT199.7 .C45 2007
736.4

To learn more about the other great books from Fox Chapel Publishing, or to find
a retailer near you, call toll-free 800-457-9112 or visit us at *www.FoxChapelPublishing.com*.

**Note to Authors:** We are always looking for talented authors to write new books in our area
of woodworking, design, and related crafts. Please send a brief letter describing your idea to
Acquisition Editor, Fox Chapel Publishing, 1970 Broad Street, East Petersburg, PA 17520.

Printed in China
First printing
Second printing

*In honor of*
THE BIRCH TREE.

# PREFACE

All inspiring ideas find a beginning somewhere. As I remember it, the vision for this book first emerged in a wood shop amidst the organic realities of wood chips, hand tools, and laughter. Active learning and exploration were under way, and half-carved wooden bowls sat on top of workbenches and chopping blocks. Nearby, the woodstove radiated affirming warmth. Outside the windows, light sparkled on water, and the far-reaching horizon of Lake Superior beckoned, its presence stretching outward and connecting us to the innumerable waterways that weave together the northern landscapes.

It was 2004, and a young nonprofit named North House Folk School was somewhere in the midst of its seventh year. Ideas for celebrating a distant but intriguing milestone (North House's tenth anniversary) were the subject of conversation. One proposal surfaced—a *festschrift*, or celebration book. In our mind's eye, it would bring alive the beauty, inspiration,

North House
Folk School campus.

and value of traditional craft while also capturing the lifelong necessity of learning. We looked at the wood chips scattered on the floor all around us and at the firewood fueling the stove that warmed us and realized a focus for our book: birch. The tree's elegant lines, circumpolar presence, rich history, and ecological story beckoned like the distant horizon.

For centuries, the northern forests and landscapes provided the elemental resources for northern cultures. Transportation, shelter, food, storage, clothing—all were truly a function of the resources at hand. Thus, the interconnection between all things living was central to life's daily rhythms. The birch tree's bark, wood, sap, and more were invaluable assets throughout the North.

Today, for better or worse, this direct connection between the landscapes we call home and our lives no longer exists. Distant resources in many forms now have redefined how we lead our lives. Thus, our ability to appreciate and truly understand the resources that surround us is no longer a function of our daily needs and instead is only a function of our ability to explore, listen, understand, and sense in new ways. To a degree, we aspire to relearn what has already been known. The hands-on process of engaging in traditional crafts is a powerful medium for reforging these connections.

People are inevitably the foundation of any dynamic organization. At North House, the talents of our artisan instructors are the sparks that ignite our exploration. The curiosity and creativity of our entire extended community is like fuel in a campfire, generating warmth, light, and sustenance that bring people together to learn and grow. Just as the collective efforts of visionary people launched North House on its journey in 1997, the cooperative and purposeful efforts of the artisans featured in this book start another shared journey on its way. It is our hope that it, too, will offer opportunities for inspiration, reflection, and exploration.

—Greg Wright
North House Folk School Executive Director

North House
Folk School

Welcome

Woodworking

Boat Building

# CONTENTS

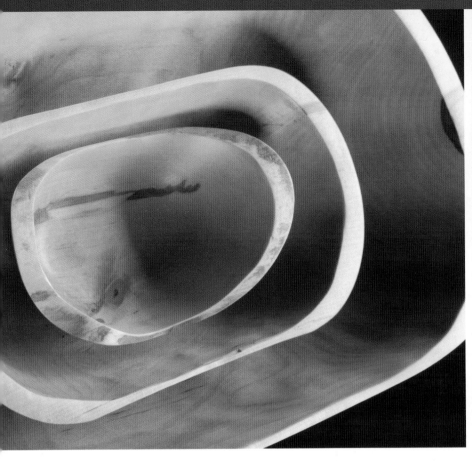

*left*
Nest of birch bowls, hand carved from green (fresh) birch log. Erv Berglund, Minnesota, 2006.

*right*
*Birch Bark Pack.* Weaving based upon traditional Finnish pack basket. Charlie Mayo, Wisconsin, 1968.

# SPONTANEOUS COMBUSTION:

## *Reminiscing about the Beginnings of North House Folk School with Founder Mark Hansen*

### BETSY BOWEN, ANNE PRINSEN, AND SCOTT POLLOCK

North House Folk School is located in the small picturesque village of Grand Marais, Minnesota, on the north shore of Lake Superior. We are geographically closer to rugged Canada than to most of Minnesota. Here within the cluster of brightly painted wooden buildings on the harbor, a student of any age can learn in a small class to build a boat or a timber frame building, or to make a rustic wooden ale bowl by hand, paint decorative traditional Nordic designs on it, and even brew the beer to drink from it. We began ten years ago with one kayak-building class, one instructor, and 12 students and now host 249 classes, 91 instructors, and over 1,200 students from 33 states and five countries over the course of a year.

We believe that the point is not so much what object is made, but the experience. Our mission states that we "inspire the heart, hands, and mind." We know that what people take away from here is not just a bowl, but a visceral and immediate experience of being part of the human community.

As we began to celebrate our first ten years by working on this book, we wondered what kind of unquenchable spark of faith and energy fired this spontaneous combustion. So we interviewed Mark Hansen, boat builder, woodworker, and instructor, to learn more about what the North House Folk School project meant to him in the early years:

———— ◆ ————

"THIS IS ABOUT PEOPLE FEELING SUCCESSFUL.
This curiosity is a result of a society that's just gone specialized. And as people, we're wired up to make shelter, food, and clothing just as our ancestors did. So there's value in that. That stimulates the brain and the senses in ways that are really important.

"After the first kayak class I taught, I had a father and son combination who came up to me after the class, and the father broke down crying, in that it had changed his life, and it had

*North House Folk School*
## MISSION

Enriching lives and building community by teaching traditional northern crafts in a student-centered learning environment that inspires the hands, the heart, and the mind.

Five basic tenets guide all programs and classes at the Folk School:

- Create a rich, positive environment that inspires lifelong learning in a noncompetitive setting.
- Help students recognize and develop their creativity, talents, and interests in a student-centered environment.
- Promote and preserve the knowledge, skills, crafts, and stories of the past and present.
- Foster the concept of intergenerational learning.
- Provide creative and meaningful opportunities for individuals, families, and groups.

changed his relationship with his son—he was emotionally just letting it all out. And it was great. It was just great."

Mark moved to Grand Marais in 1980 with his wife, Wendy, and son, Dan, to live near Lake Superior. Though he worked as a social worker, he was never far from an absorbing hands-on experience—building boats, skis, an elevator for Dan's wheelchair.

"In 1996," Mark says, "I was teaching boat building for the local community education program, down at the Coast Guard boathouse. It was twelve people the first year and fourteen people the second year from the community and regionwide. I pretty much put together a kit for different sizes—students were all the way from elementary school through retirement age. It kind of became an event—people from town came down. A lot of people had never been down to the Coast Guard building—it's a really nice building—yeah, it's the people's building; we own it. It was a lot of fun."

❦

THE CONCEPT OF A FOLK SCHOOL, and the philosophy of hands-on, equality-based learning, came to Mark through his family and his travels:

"I'd been to Norway several times and seen schools over there, and I was aware of [Niikolaj Frederik Severin] Grundtvig [an educator]—my grandfather was into Grundtvig and his philosophies—he [my grandfather] was a Lutheran minister. I thought about Grundtvig when I was formulating my ideas for this thing, read a lot of his writings, poems that he'd written, and was very impressed with his approach to education. There was a beauty

*below*
Busy students during a North House course.

*right top*
Mark Hansen, North House founder.

*right bottom*
The Schooner Hjordis, North House's classroom on the water.

"I was part of Mark's first class. I'd never built a kayak before, much less anything. I'd work during the day, take calls from the Coast Guard shed, running up from time to time to the hospital. Building the kayak was empowering to all of us; as the month progressed, we worked harder and longer and later into the evening, pushed on by the progress of our neighbors. That first launching was a community event—twelve boats thrust into the East Bay like newly hatched ducks. Mark taught a second class the next spring. That summer, North House was born."
—*Dr. John Wood, physician and former Board President*

"It was like family. Little potlucks all the time. It was a humanities class, really."
—*Mike Schelmeske, woodworker and instructor*

in it in that there were no rules about how you did it—it was a loving process, about people."

The ideas of respect for the dignity of each person and noncompetitive, uplifting learning experiences echoed strongly in Mark as he, with others, developed the philosophical base for North House Folk School:

"We just got rid of competition—which was perfect for me, because I have never been competitive. When people start to compete, I just walk away. The whole thing about grades and stars has always been to me just so much bull. My son, Dan, went to Montessori school and had a wonderful experience. It was a great school—he loved it—and then he had to go to kindergarten. He came home the first day of kindergarten saying, 'How come everyone else got a Snickers bar and I didn't?' It was because he couldn't work the scissors to make the cut—and so I was bound and determined to put this school together, to put a star on the map. We're going to do a noncompetitive school here. None of these grades or snobbishness. None of that stuff. This is going to be about enjoying people."

REAL HUMAN LIFE

Niikolaj Frederik Severin Grundtvig, 1783–1872, advocated for the creation of a unique school that would serve the Danish people at all levels in society that would be of and for the people. His special passion was that these folk schools would give dignity to the life of the farmer. They would awaken a love of learning that would continue long after a student had finished the formal course of study. In his remarks to his first group of eight students, Grundtvig said, "I saw life, real human life, as it is lived in this world, and saw at once that to be enlightened, to live a useful and enjoyable human life, most people did not need books at all, but only a genuinely kind heart; sound common sense; a kind, good ear; a kind, good mouth; and then liveliness to talk with really enlightened people who would be able to arouse their interest and show them how human life appears when the light shines upon it." *

NORTH HOUSE'S SENSE OF VALUE IN COMMUNITY evolved into a long-term relationship with the City of Grand Marais. In 1996, the city had taken possession of land and buildings on the harbor that had been owned and developed since the 1930s by the U.S. Forest Service. After considering proposals from various established community groups, North House Folk School was awarded rental of this property through a month-by-month lease, now proceeding as a long-term partnership. The city took a risk before there was much to show. As Mark remembers:

"Basically, they said go ahead. I wasn't surprised; I knew it would go—most of those classes pulled off. We had a big open house in May of 1997 and put together a board of directors. We had fiber and woodworking and birch bark, and then ran around the state and plugged it.

"It was just months and months of cleaning; it was just dirty; it was a mess. We worked mostly out of the Red Building; there was a little carpentry shop on the end, and then in the fall, we went over to the Blue Building and started there. It was pretty ragtag.

"We worked from seven in the morning until ten o'clock at night, every day, cleaning, teaching classes . . . there was always someone down there helping out."

* Steven M. Borish, *The Land of the Living: The Danish Folk High Schools and Denmark's Non-Violent Path of Modernization* (Nevada City: Blue Dolphin Publishing Inc., 1991).

North House seems to be built on faith and enthusiasm. As Mark explains:

"Why did people dive in? I think people were interested in what was going to come up next. There was always something being cooked up—we'd have staff meetings every day for three hours. There was fighting, and napping, and hanging out in the evenings. It was fun, you know. There was excitement, anticipation—'Wow, this is our space now; how do we do something with this?' It was a time you could never think of replicating. I thought, 'I'll give it full blast here for three, four years, then someone else can do it.' I wanted to have a place where I could teach and learn, without leaving town. So there were clearly selfish motives."

*top*
Hand planes in North House's wood shop.

*bottom*
The workshop woodstove.

I N LARGE PART, it was Mark's obsession and commitment to the idea that made it happen. As local supporter Buck Benson recalls, "Once Mark started rolling on the North House project, he couldn't talk about anything else. He would find a way to turn the conversation around. I thought I'd lost a friend."

And what about Mark's family during the intense startup time?

"Wendy was part of lots of conversations," Mark says. "I went part-time on my job; then I left my job, a retirement plan and all, so she earned all the money for the family. I said, 'I think I should do this,' and she said, 'Yup, we're going to do it.'

"A lot of instructors were calling us wanting to teach here. That was a great surprise. The other surprise was all the volunteer hours that people put in, people from the churches, from the town, people that are still coming down—they come down, haul stuff, scrub stuff. It was a big surprise. But we were all volunteering, and when you do that, something that is for the common good, you stand on holy ground. And you can ask people for money for something other than yourself. And they feel honored that they are being asked. We just did a lot of begging, with the philosophy that if the whole thing failed, we could always say we're sorry and we should have known better than to think we could do something like this. This is big medicine."

And now ten years later?

"Yeah, oh gosh yes, I still feel the enthusiasm here. I have a good time teaching. But would I do it again—the school? Now? I don't think I'd have the energy to do it now. I sure am glad I did it. Oh yeah, it was definitely worth it. In ten years, I've had hundreds and hundreds of students. Made, like, thirty boats here. It's been a busy ten years."

"One of my clearest memories of North House's early days is of Mark sitting at the kitchen table putting together a list of classes, calling instructors, and arranging dates and times for a school that did not yet exist. Days later, a catalog was printed featuring twenty-some classes such as reindeer handling and kantele [a Finnish musical instrument] making with photographs and course descriptions, and still no confirmed location or building to house any of it. It was then that I knew this thing was going to happen. There would be no stopping it! The idea of a folk school, a people's school, that would preserve our rich northern culture through hands-on, noncompetitive learning really ignited the imaginations of so many talented people. It felt to me like spontaneous combustion. Skilled crafters, organizers, office managers, seafarers, educators showed up ready to volunteer their time. North House had a way of using every bit of talent of all who came its way—and it still does."
—*Wendy Hansen, volunteer*

"The lively conversations and happy activity that pervade North House were there right from the start. The thing I remember the most about preparing for the first classes was the 'sweat equity' of so many people who had caught the 'NHFS Bug,' many hours of sweeping and shoveling and disposing of debris."
—*Peter Barsness, instructor and former Director*

"Before the name, before the location, the concept just made sense. Offer people an opportunity to make stuff—it just wasn't out there; it wasn't happening. That first catalog, with maybe twenty-two courses, was published without having a home. And the optimism of it, it made sense; it was about the opportunity."
—*Tom Healy, instructor and former Executive Director*

# ON A MISTY MORNING:

## *Birch throughout the Ages*

HARLEY REFSAL

IT IS STILL DARK when my alarm clock goes off, but I don't mind being roused early. I camped out here in the woods for a reason: I wanted to see, feel, hear, and smell the arrival of daylight. Normally, back in the city, I'd long for those extra five or ten minutes of sleep. Not today. I traveled up here to the North Country to get away from my usual routine. After enrolling in a five-day course in Scandinavian-style spoon carving at North House Folk School, I decided to include this little side adventure as well. I would sleep out here in the forest at least one night in order to drink in the sounds and sights of the early morning.

It's eerily quiet. No birds. No motor vehicles off in the distance. Profoundly quiet. Curled up in my down-filled sleeping bag, I feel as if I'm lying on sacred ground.

There's heavy dew. The air feels moist and cold as I breathe, and I can't see very far into the woods around me. I can see that a couple of the trees are birch. The others blend into the early morning darkness. With their dark-colored bark, they could be any number of other varieties that cover these

hills of northern Minnesota. But clad in their distinctive white bark, these queens of the forest reach out through the morning mist as if having something to tell or show me. And I respond, following mental images that peel away the centuries and millennia . . . back into the deep mists of other times and faraway places.

———————◆———————

I SEE LARGE, ROUGH HANDS kneading, softening, and forming into shape a substance that resembles tar or black modeling clay. It's harder than clay, so these hands have to press very firmly. They're molding clumps of birch bark pitch or tar, mixed with beeswax. Amazing! I'm observing the formation of the first synthetic, the first man-made product ever created—predating even pottery.

Who are these guys? They're Neanderthals, living in what is now known as Saxony-Anhalt, Germany, 45,000 to 48,000 years ago in the Middle Paleolithic Age.

Yes, birch tar, made by superheating birch bark in an airtight container, has been around for a long time—just ask the Greeks. Many, many millennia after the time of the Neanderthals, Greeks used birch tar to line (and therefore waterproof) the interior of some of their pots. Mixed with other materials such as beeswax to form an adhesive, birch tar was also used to repair broken pot handles: prehistoric superglue.

Birch . . . In Greece? Yes. Before the last massive glaciers of the Northern Hemisphere receded some 10,000 years ago, the range of birch extended much farther south than it does today. Birch forests thrived in parts of what is now southern Europe,

*far left*
Hushed forest.

*left*
Birch leaves after rain.

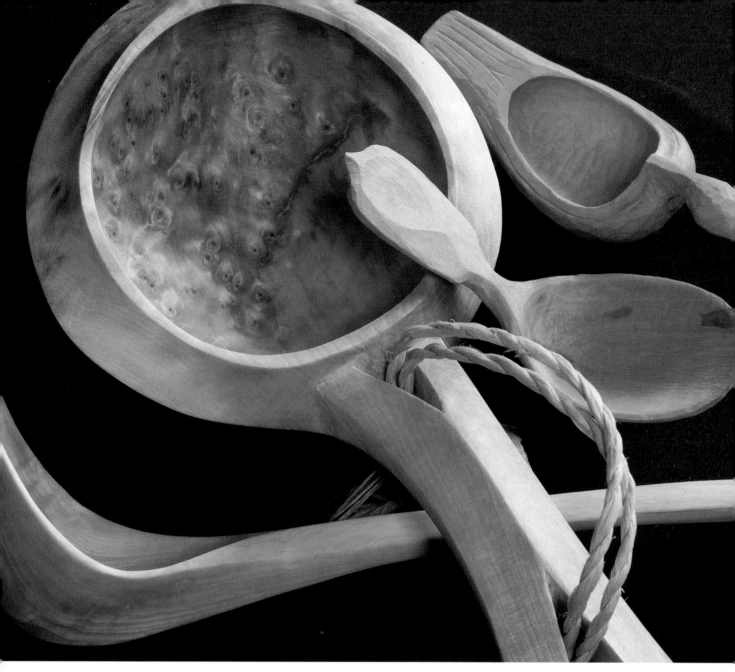

Aquavit goose, scoop, ladle, and Saami-style milk ladle, made of birch wood and root burl. Thomas Dengler, Minnesota, 2006.

and in the New World, they extended as far south as present-day Missouri.

Centuries after Greeks lined their pots with birch tar—but still more than fifty centuries ago—in approximately 3300 BC, Oetzi, the mummified Iceman discovered beside the edge of a glacier on the Austrian-Italian border in 1991, carried among his possessions two birch bark containers. One, possibly lined with fresh leaves as insulation, is thought to have contained glowing coals, enabling him to start a fire at each new campsite. The other container is thought to have held birch fungi, possibly for medicinal use. His weapons were glued to their shafts by means of birch tar.

What are some other things that gummy birch tar could be used for thousands of years ago? Chewing gum—that nasty masticating habit frequently frowned on in school—has roots deeper than our wisdom teeth.

Archaeologists in northern Europe, especially Germany and Scandinavia, have found countless black bits of tar up to 9,000 years old that feature well-defined human tooth marks, made especially by teeth of young people, aged 6 to 15. Teeth from 30- and 40-year-olds show evidence of birch tar chewing as well. Was it tasty? Did chewing tar serve as a prehistoric form of dental hygiene? Was it a stimulant of some kind? Perhaps the chewing of birch tar was just plain enjoyable.

M Y THOUGHTS RETURN to birch bark containers, like the one carried by the Iceman, Oetzi. I think of a photo I once saw of a more recent bark container than Oetzi's, excavated at a site near Trondheim, Norway, in 1927. Cylindrical like the Iceman's, it is about eight inches in diameter and six inches tall. Upon close investigation, archaeologists determined that the humble container had lain buried in that spot—formerly a moist bog—for approximately 2,500 years. The container had once held butter.

Who buried it in that bog twenty-five centuries ago? Why? Was it a religious sacrifice of some kind—an offering of butter, a symbol of plenty, a symbol of fruits of the earth—offered back to Mother Earth or other deities about whom we can only speculate?

Was the container, as Norwegian craftsman and writer Johann Hopstad* suggests, possibly placed there by a woman who wanted to conceive and bear a child? Was it made as an offering to the gods in hopes of having her wish fulfilled? Or was the bog simply a convenient, nearby prehistoric refrigerator—a place where butter, a rather precious commodity, could be stored without turning rancid?

We can only theorize about the motive, the circumstances, and the person responsible for its placement in this spot. But what we do know is that despite 2,500 years of burial in a moist bog, the container remained in remarkably good condition.

Throughout Norway, other buried birch bark containers have also been found. A 2,300-year-old container found in a stone quarry in the county of Hedmark in the 1960s reveals how the container was stitched. Another lid from a Norwegian container dating from around 1000 AD features a geometric decorative design engraved into the birch bark with a stylus.

Thousands of miles away, long-buried birch bark shared yet another fascinating story. In 1881, a farmer near the village of Bakhshali (then in northern India, now situated in Pakistan) began to

* Johann Hopstad, *Never* (Oslo: Landbruksforlaget A/S, 1990), 9.

build a rock retaining wall. As he dug, he unearthed some odd-looking bits of material. Birch bark—lots of it—bound together into a bundle.

Close examination, first by a local law enforcement officer, then by academic specialists, began to tell an exciting tale, especially for mathematicians. The so-called Bakhshali Manuscript is a scholarly paper or treatise, written on some seventy sheets of birch bark, discussing, among other concepts, the groundbreaking use of zero in mathematical calculations. Many scholars date the manuscript, now in the British Museum, to the third or fourth century AD.

Manuscripts scratched into pressure-sensitive birch bark have been discovered in other places as well. A fifth-century manuscript found in Afghanistan sheds light on the history of early Buddhism.

And in Russia—especially in Novgorod, a city located between St. Petersburg and Moscow—birch bark manuscripts have been excavated by the hundreds, dating from the eleventh through the fifteenth centuries.

Large birch bark shoes. John Zasada, Minnesota, 2006.

*above top*
Replica Montreal canoe. Grand Portage National Monument, Minnesota, 2005.

*above bottom*
Winter birch bark basket incised with floral decoration. Artist unknown. Loan courtesy of Grand Portage National Monument.

from speeches and correspondence written by well-known Novgorod statesmen to notes written by young schoolchildren. Birch bark was free and readily available material on which to write. One could use ink and simply write on the bark, or scribe words, letters, or symbols with a stylus, which could have been as simple as a pointed stick.

At the same time folks were writing on birch bark in Novgorod, their neighbors to the west were putting the versatile material to yet another use. Norway, in the early 1200s, was in a state of nearly constant civil war. Two main groups vied for control of the country. One of the factions was called the Baglers, a powerful dynasty or clan that hailed from the area east of present-day Lillehammer, near the Norwegian-Swedish border. Their rivals, a poor, disparate, but highly dedicated group, were known as the Birkebeiner, or Birch-Legs—a name given to them because many were so poor that they couldn't afford winter clothing; instead, they wrapped birch bark around their legs and feet as footwear and for warmth.

In 1204, King Haakon Sverresson, a Birkebeiner, died, leaving only an infant son, Haakon Haakonsson, as the heir to his throne. The Baglers, hoping to gain the throne, set out to capture and kill the baby. So on Christmas Day 1205, two of the best skiers among the Birkebeiners bundled up the young prince, wrapped their own legs in birch bark, and set off on a daunting ski trip through the Norwegian mountains to bring their precious cargo to safety in the city of Trondheim.

The trip was a success. The Birkebeiners arrived safely in Trondheim in early 1206, and the baby survived the trip, growing up to become King Haakon Haakonsson. King Haakon successfully ended the civil wars and during his long reign brought peace and stability to the country.

In commemoration of that memorable ski trip and its historic consequences, organizers in Norway established the Birkebeiner Ski Race in 1932, an annual event that continues to this day. Participants

Among the manuscripts was the first personal letter to contain obscene words. A resident of Staraya, Russia, wrote a letter to his brother, urging him—to put it mildly—not to show off in his trade business. Unfortunately, this obscene birch bark letter had no signature. Historians believe that if the author of this letter could have known that it would be found a thousand years later, he would have signed it and gone down in Russian history as the first "official ribald."*

The writers of the Novgorod birch bark manuscripts and letters were a diverse lot. Documents discovered to date include everything

* Unknown, "Reporter's Note-Book: First Birch Bark Letter was Found in Veliky Novgorod 51 Years Ago," *Pravda On-line* (July 26, 2002).

ski a course of 54 kilometers (approximately 32½ miles) that runs from the community of Rena to Lillehammer, a portion of the trail the original Birkebeiners traveled on their way to Trondheim. Each skier must wear a backpack weighing at least 3.5 kilograms (approximately 8 pounds), symbolizing the weight of the young Prince Haakon. The race has even crossed the Atlantic Ocean: The annual Wisconsin-based Birkebeiner, often referred to as the "Birkie," began in 1973. And more recently, the Rena/Lillehammer event has also been joined by a Canadian-based Birkebeiner.

The original Birkebeiners made use of a material that was all around them. Birch bark was a highly valued material even then; the right to harvest birch bark was even encoded in law. The National Code of Laws, adopted by King Magnus Lagaboter (Magnus the Lawmender), was written sometime before 1267 AD.

IN ADDITION to the uses cited above, birch bark, with its impressive rot-resistant qualities, is used for everything from outdoor building materials to components in musical instruments, from colorant for dyeing yarn to food additives. In times of famine, finely ground bark was added to flour in order to stretch the precious supply to make it last longer. The resulting bread was called bark bread.

There was a time when birch bark cultures used birch bark as a trade good. One could pay taxes with birch bark. Records from 1820 show that a farmer near Kongsvinger, Norway, paid his veterinary bill with birch bark.

And then there was also the so-called birch bark mile—the distance a person could walk in a pair of woven birch bark shoes before wearing through them. That distance? About 16 kilometers (approximately 9½ miles). No wonder folks walking a longer distance took along some birch bark strips to make shoe repairs—or an extra pair of birch bark

# BIRCH SKIS
*Mark Hansen, North House founder and instructor*

The ski is an ancient tool used by a variety of cultures to travel the frozen North. The prehistoric origins of the ski date at least 2,500 years ago. In an old Ural dialect, the Saami people were described as the *skidfinnars*, or the "fast travelers" of the North.

Skis have been made from the wood of many types of trees throughout Scandinavia and Siberia, but the birch tree has a growth range and unique qualities that made it a dominant species for ski construction. The birch has a cell structure referred to as long grain, in that it is fibrous and stringy, making it amenable to bending and offering a high degree of flexibility.

Many types and varieties of skis have been made throughout the North. These types have depended on intended use, snow conditions, and terrain, as well as cultural and traditional differences. The evolution of the ski has brought many changes in its shape, size, and methods of construction. What has remained constant is the use of the birch tree for the construction of many skis—including its modern use as a wood core for the laminated recreational ski.

*above*
Antler-tipped ski pole. Mark Hansen, Minnesota, 2005.

*right*
(left to right) Church skis, Telemark style. Saami-style skis. Mark Hansen, Minnesota, 2005.

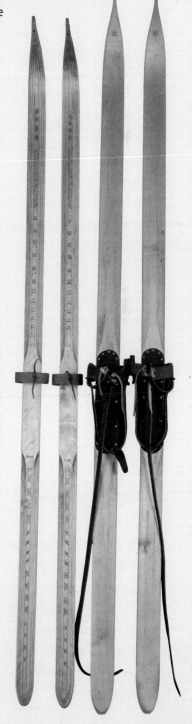

# BIRCH-SPLITTIN' BITTER, ICICLE-LICKIN' SWEET ROOT BEER

Brewed by the Unofficial North House Folk School Brew Club on the Sixth of March in the Year 2006 in Celebration of the Birch.

## INGREDIENTS:

- 3 qt. birch sap
- 1 qt. water
- ½ c. sassafras root bark
- 2 dried apple slices
- 15 raisins
- ¼" whole vanilla bean
- ¼ tsp. ground licorice root
- Small bundle of yellow birch or paper birch twigs
- ½ c. brown sugar
- 4 oz. birch syrup
- ¼ tsp. champagne yeast

## PROCESS:

In a large saucepan, bring the birch sap and water to a boil. Add the sassafras root bark, apple slices, raisins, vanilla bean, and licorice root. Lower the heat and simmer for 25 minutes. If using yellow birch twigs, add the bundle at the start of the boil. If using paper birch twigs, add the bundle 10 minutes before the end of the simmer. Turn off the heat and stir in the brown sugar and birch syrup. Strain into a different container. Add the yeast and agitate or stir it in. Bottle and cap the mixture. Let it sit for up to 48 hours at room temperature. Refrigerate the root beer immediately and drink it within two weeks (keep it refrigerated or the bottles may explode as $CO_2$ is released at room temperature when yeasts eat sugars).

shoes. Housewives in preindustrial rural Finland used to make dozens of pairs of birch bark shoes each year in order to keep their families in footwear.

When the winter was long and the summer grass was late in arriving, farmers in Scandinavia and Russia often kept their cattle alive by feeding them birch twigs. Birch trees were some of the first species to leaf out in the spring, and the tender green leaves and shoots, although perhaps not as convenient a fodder as pasture grass, often spelled the difference between starvation and salvation for cattle until pasture grass was once again available.

---

I T'S GROWN LIGHTER NOW. Although my forest-floor bedroom is still a little hazy, objects and details are coming more clearly into focus. As I admire the white pillars around me and follow the trunks up to the branches and leaves gently swaying in the wind, I remember that I'm surrounded by royalty. The birch is the sweetheart of every country in which it grows.

---

M ANY OF THE DESCENDANTS of those birch-bark-culture Europeans eventually immigrated to the New World. Those who settled in the northernmost Midwestern and Northeastern regions of the lower 48—as well as in Canada and Alaska—were undoubtedly delighted to encounter the beautiful, versatile "giving tree" with which they were already familiar.

They also encountered indigenous populations: First Nation people. Native Americans. People who had long and rich traditions of their own when it came to the birch tree and its uses. Many lived in birch bark dwellings, gathered berries, and boiled water in birch bark containers. There was also the birch bark canoe—perhaps the most emblematic feature of New World birch bark culture.

When French explorers, and later, fur traders, laid eyes on North American birch bark canoes, they recognized immediately that they were looking at a better model than the watercraft with which they were familiar. These beauties were riverworthy, durable, repairable en route, fast, and best of all, light enough to portage from one river or body of water to another. Technological marvels, they quickly became the watercraft of choice, and the picturesque birch bark canoe has been immortalized through literature, drawings, paintings, and photographs.

———— ◆ ————

WHY HAVE I BEEN thinking so much about birch bark? Bark is, after all, only one product of the birch tree. What about the wood itself? The leaves, the roots, and the sap? Haven't those parts of the tree been as useful throughout history as the bark has been? Well, yes, they've all been valuable. But they've not had the same staying power.

As I look around the forest floor, I can see several fallen birch trees. What remains of the tree is a hollow tube of somewhat darkened white bark. It reminds me of a large, white cardboard mailing tube. Its original contents have rotted away, leaving only the bark tube behind. That's why a four- to five-inch-wide strip of birch bark, tightly coiled into a cylinder shape, made an ideal water-resistant float when tied to a fishnet. And conversely, strips of birch bark were wrapped around stones and tied to fishnets to keep them submerged.

Yes, the wood from the tree was valuable as well. It provided material for buildings, vehicles, farm machinery, tools, and firewood. Spoons, whether meant for everyday use or fancy courtship gifts, were carved from birch. Skis, ski bindings, snowshoes for horses, fences, buckets, wooden shoes, eating and serving utensils, furniture . . . These compose only a small list of the many and varied uses of birch wood.

Young, dense paper birch tree stand in northern Minnesota.

And how about decorating? Birch twigs, with leaves attached, are common decorations in Scandinavia. Vases filled with birch twigs, together with wildflowers, national flags, or colored ribbons, decorate countless midsummer party venues in Sweden, Finland, and Russia, as well as May 17 (Constitution Day) celebrations in Norway.

———— ◆ ————

SO SHE IS OF ROYAL SAP, this queen of the forest. Where does she go from here? Lately, she offers her wood for making paper, plywood, and paneling.

Some of her bark may be turned into cosmetic products, due to its high betulin content. Other parts of the tree will be lovingly crafted into birch bark containers, skis, fences, bowls, and Scandinavian-style spoons.

———— ◆ ————

IT'S TIME TO GET UP and head off to my first day of class. Celebrating birch.

# BIRCH BARK

"WE CANNOT LEAVE A CONSIDERATION
OF THE BARK WITHOUT MENTIONING ITS
SEEMINGLY 'MAGICAL' PROPERTIES . . ."
—*John Zasada, forester and instructor*

The birch tree's many parts—including its wood, leaves, roots, and sap—have proved useful to people throughout history. Yet it is the bark that stands out among the tree's many gifts. With attributes ranging from its rot- and water-resistance to its sheer beauty, birch bark can be used to create containers, shoes, dye, canoes, and a variety of other items as shown on the following pages.

# Condensed Smoke:
# BIRCH TAR

## MARK HANSEN

Mark initially learned about the process of boiling birch tar while studying boat building in Norway. "It would be a process of several days," says Mark. "While the tar was dripping, everyone would eat and drink and have a merry time." Birch tar can be used on skis and boats and to treat leather. It's really just condensed smoke—a preservative that stops mildew and prevents rot.

## Materials

- 2½ to 3 qt. empty metal can, approx. 6" tall x 6" diameter, such as a 3 lb. coffee can

- Enough strips of fine birch bark to tightly pack the 2½ to 3 qt. metal can

- Discarded metal road sign or piece of sheet metal, approx. 2-ft. square

- Electric drill and ¼" bit

- Hammer

- Low, widemouthed empty metal can, approx. 1½" tall x 3" diameter, such as a tuna can

- Rocks

- Sand

- Wood shavings

- Firewood

- Matches

1. Coil the birch bark strips into a 2½ to 3 qt. metal can until the can is tightly packed (A).

2. Drill a ¼" hole, ideally in the center of a road sign or sheet metal, and slightly dish the area around the hole with a hammer, creating a slight funnel through which the liquid tar can flow (B). If you don't have a clear space in the center, you can drill the hole off center as I have. Place the open can upside down directly over the drilled hole.

3. Dig a small hole in the ground large enough for a low, widemouthed metal can to sit within. Place the low can open side up in the hole.

4. Place the road sign and the 2½ to 3 qt. can directly over the lower can, carefully aligning the drilled hole over the buried can below.

5. Weight down the 2½ to 3 qt. can with a couple of rocks (C). Place sand around the base and on the sign, creating an airtight gasket (D).

6. Around and on top of the 2½ to 3 qt. can, build a fire (E–G). Allow it to burn for half an hour. Make certain the fire burns evenly the entire time and around the entire can so it chars all of the bark inside (H–I).

7. After a half hour has passed, sweep only the ashes away from the 2½ to 3 qt. can, leaving them buried in sand. Allow the road sign time to cool completely; then, remove the rocks and sand to pull the buried can out. If the bark has been charred through, you will be left with a usable quarter cup of tar. If not using it right away, store the birch tar in a lidded container.

E

F

G

H

I

## A Silk Scarf Kissed with Bark:
# BIRCH DYE

### LARRY SCHMITT

This natural dye project is done without the more common method of a dye pot over a fire because it's safer, easier, and can be done in classrooms or outdoors at a picnic table. However, eliminating the heat means that the dye process can take longer. It is also possible that some intensity of color will be lost without the use of heat, and there is the possibility that the natural materials used as dye sources could start to decompose and even ferment during the extended period required for dyeing. The fiber selected for dyeing must be highly receptive to dyes and also resistant to decomposition—silk is an obvious choice.

### Materials

- Silk scarf in neutral color
- Strips or pieces of birch bark, (papery outer bark, brittle red-brown inner bark, or both)
- Other dye materials, such as red plant matter, juices, condiments, herbs, or spices
- Handful or less of iron, copper, or aluminum modifiers, such as old hardware or pennies (optional)
- 12" piece of steel wire or nylon, polyester, or acrylic string or yarn
- Sturdy plastic bag or disposable container
- 2 Tbsp. to ½ c. vinegar, wine, or fruit juice
- Large dishpan
- Protective gloves
- Mild soap or detergent
- Steam iron (optional)

## A NOTE ABOUT MATERIALS

Let's take a look at some of the materials specific to dyeing. The first thing you'll need is a *sturdy plastic bag or other disposable container.* You'll also need *wire, string, or yarn* to hold the bundle together. If using string or yarn, it's a good idea to select a type that will resist decomposition, such as nylon, polyester, or acrylic.

You will also need *birch bark*. You can use the papery outer bark, the brittle red-brown inner bark, or both. The conventional wisdom for dyes that are known to produce reds is that better results are obtained by adding other materials that are also red. So look for *red plant material, blossoms, red leaves, red bark, or red roots.* Also consider the items sitting at the back of your refrigerator or pantry—*juices, condiments, herbs, spices, and herbal teas.*

*Birch leaves* harvested in spring can be used as a natural dye source for yellow dye. Many other plant materials can be used for a variety of colors. Some ideas to experiment with are *pomegranate rind, avocado seed and peel, dill, turmeric, curry powder, zinnias, black beans, and coffee.*

### MODIFIERS

Modifiers are things that will assist the natural dyes to bond onto the fabric. They may not be entirely necessary, but their use increases the possibilities. *Iron, copper, and aluminum* are all options. For iron, select anything on your workbench that looks as if it has the potential to rust—for example, wire, nails, screws, nuts, bolts, or steel wool. If you can find "bare steel" wire, use it! For copper, use pennies, copper wire, copper pipe, or even brass knickknacks. For aluminum, use antiperspirants; they contain aluminum compounds.

### LIQUID

Liquid is required to assist in transferring color from the dye material to the fabric. If you are using a modifier, select a liquid that is acidic—for example, *vinegar, wine, or fruit juice. Tannic acid* is well known for its ability to assist in the natural dye process. You can use *green tea, black tea, or any of the red wines* known for high tannic acid content. Or you can collect *leaves, bark, nuts, or berries from sumac or oak* to add to the liquid. We know from the early European visitors to Lake Superior that Native Americans used tannic acid from leaves and barks in their dye recipes. We also know that in certain areas along Lake Superior shores, pure iron could be found. It was collected and used for dyeing. Just outside of Grand Marais, we find outcroppings of iron-rich basaltic stone—not the pure iron that was highly prized, but rich enough to yield results with patience!

1. Spread out the dye materials and, if using, any modifiers on the silk scarf (**A–B**). Birch bark, red leaves, blossoms from the woods, and green tea (still in bags) have been arranged on half of this large scarf.

2. Fold the remainder of the scarf over and roll it up into a somewhat tight ball (**C**).

3. Wrap steel wire around the balled-up scarf (**D**).

4. Place the bundle in a plastic bag and add the vinegar—as little as 2 tablespoons or as much as ½ cup, or more (**E**). The more liquid you add, the more the colors will disperse. For more of a tie-dyed effect, use less liquid.

5. Seal the bag and place it in a dishpan so that leakage is contained (**F**). Allow two weeks for the dyeing to occur. If you used copper, open and rewrap the scarf every three or four days so that the contact with the copper is distributed. Be sure to wear protective gloves when handling the scarf. Prolonged contact with copper can lead to deterioration of the fabric. Flipping the bag over will affect the result, but it is an artistic decision, not a necessity. Watch for fermentation. If the bag starts to bloat, open it to release the gases. Store dye projects in a location out of reach of unsuspecting humans or animals.

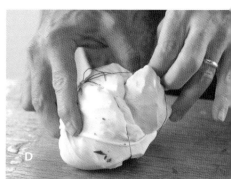

6. Two weeks later: The dye project is ready for inspection. Again, wear protective gloves when unfolding the scarf (G–J). Protect work surfaces as well.

7. If you are satisfied with the results, shake off the dye materials and spread the scarf to dry outdoors (K). When the scarf is completely dry, hang it in a closet out of the light for two more weeks. This interval of rest assists in setting the color.

8. After two weeks, the scarf can be hand washed with a mild soap. Some color may come out. Also, some natural dye materials are sensitive to changes in pH, and it is possible that the soap or detergent used will cause a shift in color even at this point. Before we had soaps and detergents, we might have soaked one part birch leaves to two parts water to create a washing solution for our dye project!

9. If you wish, iron the finished scarf (L). Silk must be wet when ironed so that it dries during the process. Using a steam setting on the iron will reduce the possibility of water spotting.

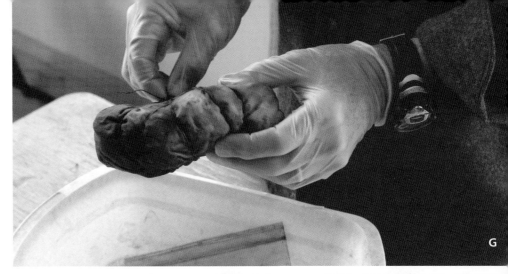

G

I

J

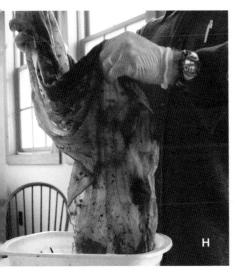

H

K

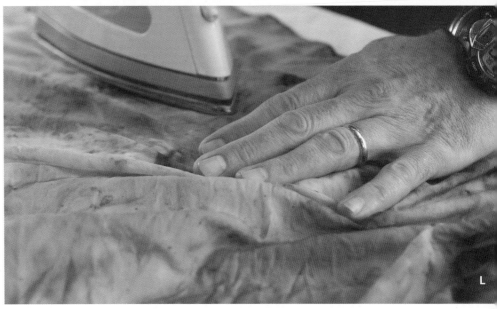

L

17

# *The Seven Deadly Sins:*
# RATTLE

## CHARLIE MAYO

In old times, this rattle was also referred to as "The Seven Deadly Sins." The rattles were made for babies at baptism time, and each stone placed within the rattle represented a deadly sin. When confirmed, the children were reminded to shake the rattle during times of temptation to remind themselves of the gravity of their choices.

## *Materials*

◆ Strip of birch bark, 1" wide x 12" long

◆ 7 small pebbles

◆ Scissors

1. On one end of a 1"-wide x 12"-long birch bark strip, fold three 1" squares, accordion-style. The third square will be the most difficult to fold. Press down firmly to crease the bark. The bark is sturdy, so don't worry about breaking it (A).

2. Unfold the squares (B). You will be left with three creases.

3. Take the upper right corner and the lower right corner of the first (end) square and match them to the upper left and the upper right of the third square, respectively. This will create a cone or tent. Place seven rocks (the seven deadly sins) inside the tent (C–D).

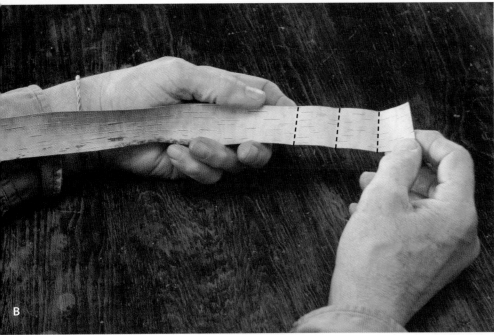

PATH

4. Fold the "path" (the remaining long tail) 90 degrees to the base of the opening to make a "door" to the tent (E). Next, wrap the "roofline" of this tent, following the roofline to the left, making certain to hold it together and not lose the sins.

5. Trim the corners of the path to form a point. The path goes between the door and the "wall" (F). Pull through the door, holding the structure together while pulling (G). Continue to wrap the side of the tent with the path to the back door (the little hole in the rear). Close the back door by inserting the path and pulling it snugly (H–J). Keep the shape of the tent. Keep the path intact as the rattle's handle.

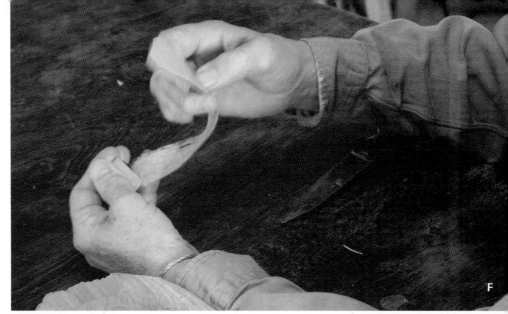

F

G

H

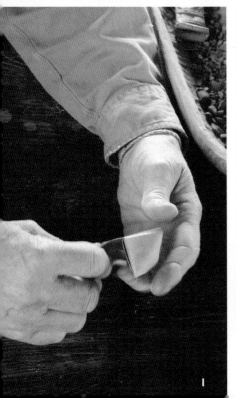

I

J

21

# *Pre-Engagement Promises:*
# RING

## CHARLIE MAYO

Finland, like her northern sisters, has always had a pragmatic and sacred relationship with the birch tree. Rings, such as the one shown in this demonstration, were often given to young Finnish girls by suitors who playfully "wedded" their brides-to-be before giving a real engagement ring. Instructor Charlie Mayo is constantly making these rings and handing them out to strangers, North House staff, and interns.

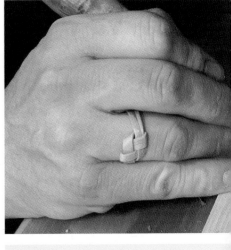

## *Materials*

- ◆ Strip of birch bark, 1" wide x 12" long
- ◆ Scissors

A

B

1. With scissors, cut a ⅜" strip from a 1" piece of bark. Use your fingers to split the narrow strip into a thinner, very flexible piece (A–C).

2. Fold the strip in two at a 45-degree angle, creating a "leg" and a "foot." The leg should be about three times as long as the foot (D).

3. Fold the leg around the foot and onto the "ankle," creating a loop (E).

4. Take the foot and wrap it over the leg and under the ankle (F). Carefully tighten. Pull the leg to size the ring (G–H).

C

D

E

F

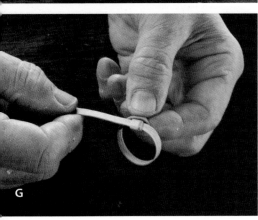

G

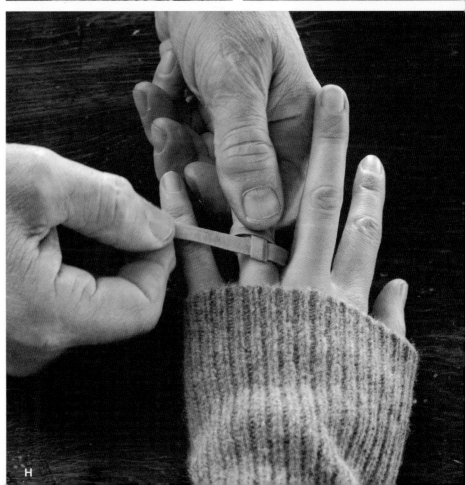

H

5. After removing the sized ring, take the leg through the ring, carefully pulling to make the new loop smaller (I–L). Pull the leg over the ring and under the new loop. Carefully tighten.

6. Tighten the knot and trim the tails (M–P). This is a Friendship knot and is tight enough to keep the ring from unraveling. Place the ring on the finger of someone you love.

I

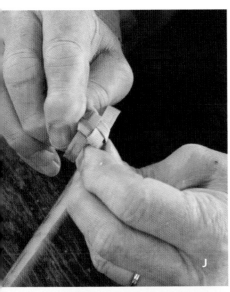

J

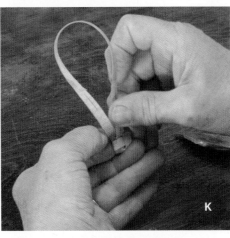

K

L

M

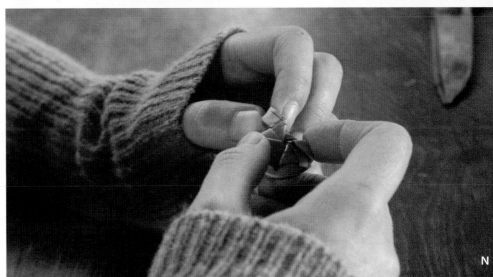

N

O

P

## *Glorify Its Color:*
# WOVEN MAT

## JOHN ZASADA

When you split bark before weaving, what you're splitting off is an annual growth layer of wood. You are stripping away—touching and feeling—the life and history of this tree, its seasons and years. Weaving is only one part of the creation process. Finding the bark and preparing it is perhaps even more important. Beeswax is often used to moisten the bark and glorify its color—and it also helps protect your hands as you work, since weaving can be pretty hard on the hands. These woven mats make great coasters, and they can be made in various sizes and weave patterns—a good way to test design ideas for bigger or more complicated projects.

## Materials

◆ 16 strips of birch bark, ¾" wide x 24" long

◆ Scissors

◆ Several clothespins

◆ Dewclaw (a butter-knife-like tool) or butter knife

A

B

1. For an 8" x 8" mat, begin with sixteen ¾"-wide x 24" long birch bark strips. With scissors, trim all the ends to a bevel. Lay out three strips, light side up, in a vertical position on the work surface. Begin the weave with two horizontal strips, dark side up (A–B). Basket weave the dark strips over and under the light strips. Build the square as you go by adding strips vertically and horizontally in the same manner and weaving along the way (C).

2. Weave until the square is set, and clothespin all the corners to keep everything in place (D–E).

3. Flip the weaving over, tighten the weave, and reclip as needed (F).

C

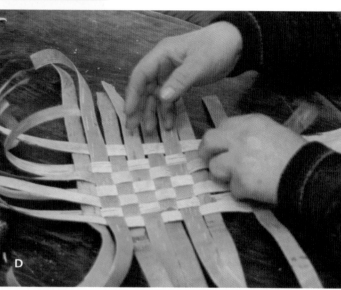

D

E

F

4. Fold the bottom right strip over all the other woven strips, and clip it with a clothespin to hold it down (G–I).

5. The strips under this fold are next folded over and tucked (J), except for the final corner strip. Fold this corner over all of the strips and follow by folding the left-hand bottom strip back over all of the strips, creating a crosspiece.

6. Repeat this "weave under" step. Trim off all the ends (K–L).

7. Rotate the square clockwise and repeat Steps 4 through 6, using a dewclaw to tighten the weave when necessary (M). Pull each strip as far as it will go and then trim. Although this woven mat looks glorious on a wooden tabletop, extremely hot dishes may burn it or alter its color.

G

H

I

J

K

L

M

# *An Instant Connection:*
# FOLDED BOX

## JOHN ZASADA

John Zasada started making things out of birch bark about ten years ago with instructor Charlie Mayo—he was in the first class that Charlie taught at North House. John had never had a hobby in his life, and it was an instant connection. If anyone had told him fifteen years ago that he'd be teaching a handcraft someday, John would have laughed, and his family certainly wouldn't have believed it.

This box is similar to those constructed in the traditional art of Chinese, Japanese, and Moorish paper folding. The birch bark serves as a sturdy, long-lasting material.

## Materials

- 2 squares of paper-thin birch bark about 9", one ⅜" larger than the other (yields a box approximately 3½")
- Extra pieces of birch bark, roughly ⅔ the size of the squares
- Scissors
- Carpenter's square
- Ruler
- Pencil
- Awl

1. Using scissors, cut two perfectly square pieces of paper-thin birch bark. One piece should be about ⅜" larger than the other. The smaller piece will be the box's bottom; the larger, the top. Use a carpenter's square to arrive at clean, square pieces (**A–D**).

2. Mark the center of both pieces by drawing an X from corner to corner using a ruler and an awl (**E**).

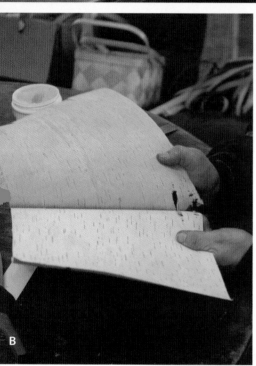

B

C

D

E

3. Using the larger piece of birch bark, fold each corner to the center point. You will arrive at a square that is smaller than the original (F).

4. Next, fold the opposite sides to the center all the way around the box. You will be left with a smaller square. Crease the folds (G).

5. Unfold the opposite sides, leaving the corners folded to the center (H). At each corner of this square will be a square. Cut the lower fold of the top two squares and the upper fold of the lower two squares, leaving two sides with long tabs (I).

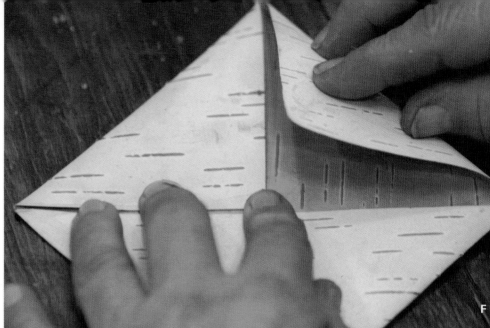

6. Fold the two sides with long tabs up. Then, fold the tabs at 90 degrees so that they are parallel with the other two sides. The two sides without tabs are then folded over, and the tabs are secured (J–N).

7. Next, trace and cut a piece of bark to fit snugly over the existing flaps. Place within the lid, trimming if necessary (O–R).

8. Follow Steps 3 through 7 for the bottom piece, and fit the top and bottom of the box together (S).

O

P

Q

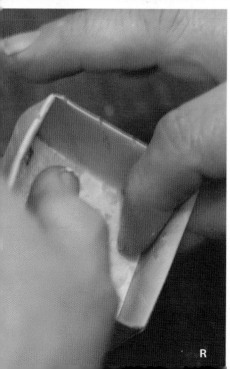

R

S

35

# *Surprises for Hands:*
# HEART BASKET

## JOHN ZASADA

Heart-shaped baskets are among the most common holiday decorations in Scandinavia—they are hung on the Christmas tree in nearly every home. The baskets, made of birch bark or paper, typically contain candy, nuts, or other surprises for big and little hands.

## Materials

- ◆ 2 rectangles of birch bark, 2" wide x 6" long
- ◆ Scissors
- ◆ Material for handle, such as birch bark, yarn, or paper
- ◆ Glue or tape

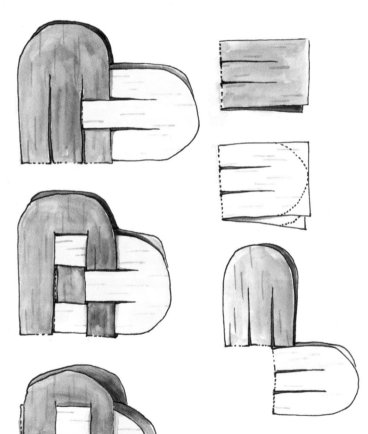

1. Cut two rectangles, 2" wide x 6" long, out of thin, flexible birch bark. Fold each in half. If the color on the two sides of the bark differs, the color pattern can be varied by folding the pieces so different colors are exposed, as I have done (A). Make two cuts in each with scissors, slightly more than 2" in from the folded edge (B).

2. Round off the open edges (the edges opposite the folded edges) using scissors (C–D).

3. Holding a folded piece of one color in each hand, weave the first butter-colored strip around a darker strip, through the next darker strip, and around the third (E).

A
B
C
D
E

4. Weave the second butter-colored strip through the first darker strip, around the second darker strip, and through the third darker strip (F).

5. Weave the final butter-colored strip just as in Step 3 (G).

6. Open the heart basket (H–I) and glue or tape a handle to the inside. Fill with nuts, candy, or other fabulous surprises.

F

H

G

I

# *As the Years Pass:*
# STAR ORNAMENT

## JULIE KEAN

The eight-pointed star has shown up often throughout history: on the oldest American quilt patterns dating back to the early 1800s; as the insignia of the National Fire Service; and as a representation of the eight seasonal pagan rituals, whose key factors are change, regeneration, and abundance.

North House holds these star ornaments dear, and each year the staff gathers during the holidays with volunteers, family, and community to make the ornaments together before sharing a meal.

## Materials

◆ 4 strips of birch bark, ¾" wide x 24" long

◆ Scissors

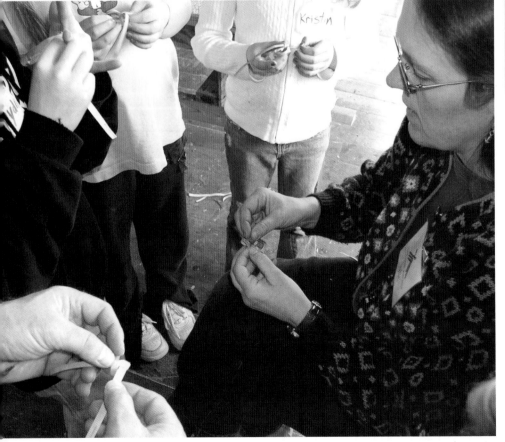

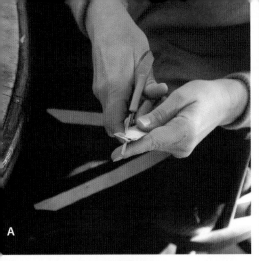

1. Start with four strips of ¾"-wide x 24"-long birch bark. Using scissors, cut a 45-degree bevel on each side of each strip (A). Fold all four strips in half (B). Slide one strip inside a second strip.

2. Slide a third strip through the initial first strip so that it lies horizontal and above the last, with its tail exiting the opposite way (C–E).

3. Weave the fourth strip over and through the third, creating a square with all of its tails pointing in different directions (F). Pull gently on all ends to tighten (G–I).

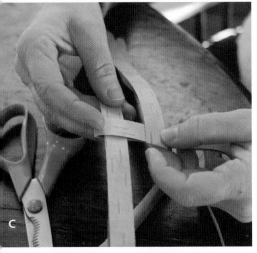

A

B

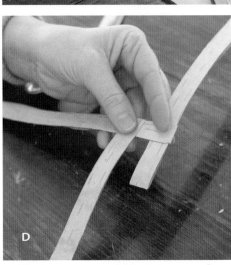

C

D

E

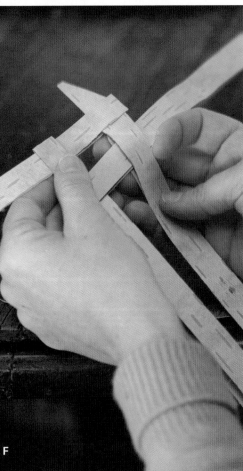

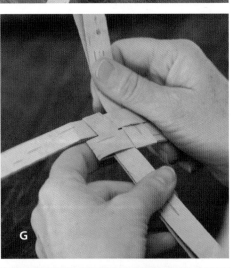

F

G

H

I

4. Flip each of the top tails over the center and fold at a 90-degree angle. The last tail goes over and tucks under the first (J–M).

5. Starting with the northwest corner of the square, the tail coming out of the open square is folded backward at a 45-degree angle (N–P) and then down in on itself (Q–S). Tuck it under.

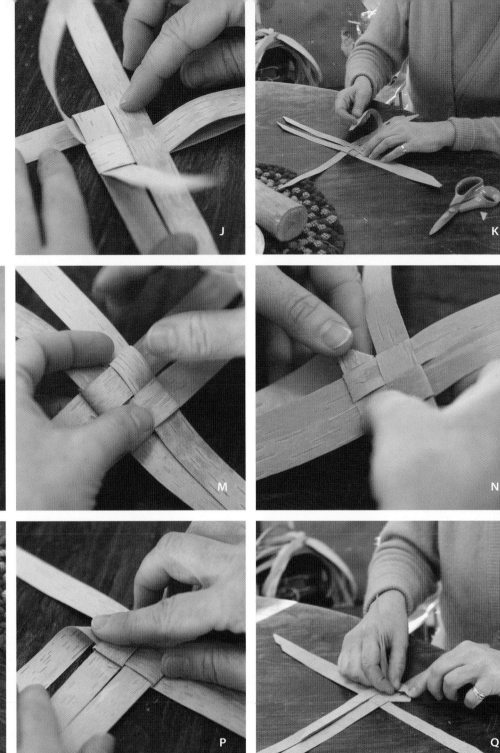

6. Fold along the final previously folded 45-degree angle forward and down to create the top of a triangle with the last fold. Fold this triangle in half to make a point (T).

7. Tuck the tail (visible in T) end under the initial first fold of the inner square, threading it through (U–W).

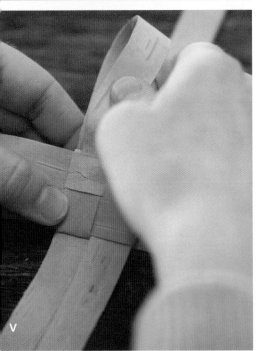

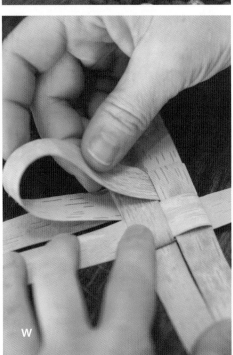

8. Repeat Steps 6 and 7 by turning the star
   90 degrees each time (X–Z) and repeating
   four times (AA). Flip the star over and repeat
   (BB–FF). You will be left with eight points.

GG

9. Twist one of the tails around, creating a loop, and insert it under the adjacent tail. Push it through until it lies tight and forms a cone. The tail will come out of the shown point (GG–HH). Do this four times. Turn the star over and repeat for the other side (II–QQ).

HH

II

JJ

KK

LL

0. Trim off any excess tails and strips, leaving just a star. Cut the tails flush to the already present angles (**RR–TT**).

MM

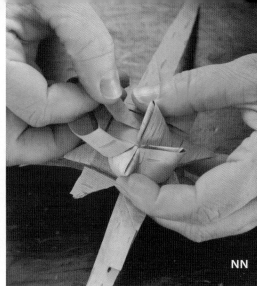

NN

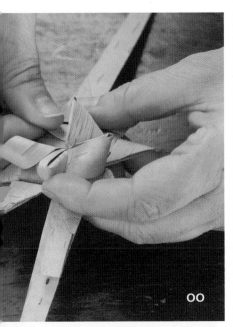

OO

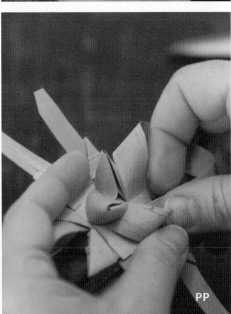

PP

QQ

RR

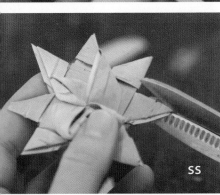

SS

TT

# *Reflecting the Life:*
# BASKET

## JULIE KEAN

The birch tree is an integral part of Julie Kean's daily life, especially because her home is in the midst of birch trees. In the winter, the wood keeps her warm, and in the summer, the birches shade her from the sun's harsh rays. She considers it a privilege to live among these trees and to be able to craft the bark into usable objects. When she crafts, she doesn't need to worry if the finished product will be beautiful because the beauty of the tree transfers to the object, as with this basket. The basket reflects the life of the tree. She feels that it is her extreme good fortune to be able to honor the birch tree with the craft that she practices.

*right and below*
Assorted woven baskets. Julie Kean, Minnesota, 2006.

## Materials

- ◆ 13 strips of birch bark, 1" wide x 12" long
- ◆ Several extra strips of birch bark, 1" wide x 12" long
- ◆ Scissors
- ◆ Several clothespins
- ◆ Fid (long narrow tool that loosens existing weave to facilitate the placement of the new weaving underneath)

A

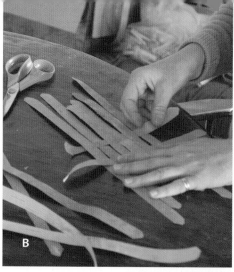

B

1. Using scissors, clip the ends of twelve of the 1"-wide x 12"-long strips of birch bark at a bev(el) (**A**). This will make weaving much easier. Set th(e) thirteenth strip aside for later.

2. Lay six strips parallel to each other, butter-colored side up. Then, weave the remaining si(x) strips, butter-colored side up, over and under the first six strips, weaving each successive stri(p) opposite the one next to it to create a basket weave (**B–C**). Tighten the looser strips, and clamp the corners with clothespins to hold the(m) strips in place (**D**).

C

D

E

F

3. Count over three strips from the corner and use the two middle strips to form a corner by weaving up (E). Continue this weaving with the remaining strips on that side (F–G). Repeat three more times to complete the other sides (H–L).

4. Count up four diamonds at each corner. Fold down the strips, and clothespin so that the strips continue to be at a diagonal (pointing down) and the edge of the basket is straight across. Repeat four times around the basket and clip (M–N).

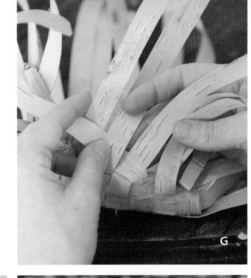

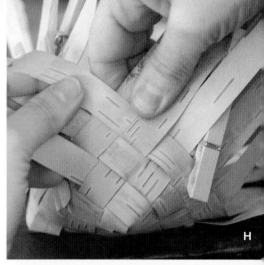

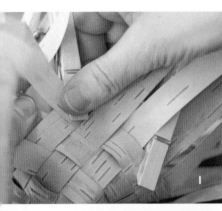

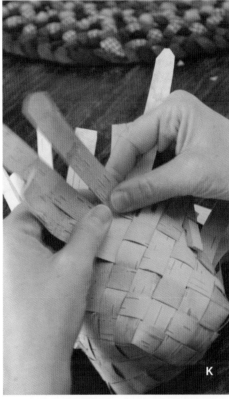

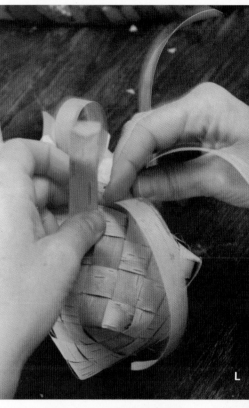

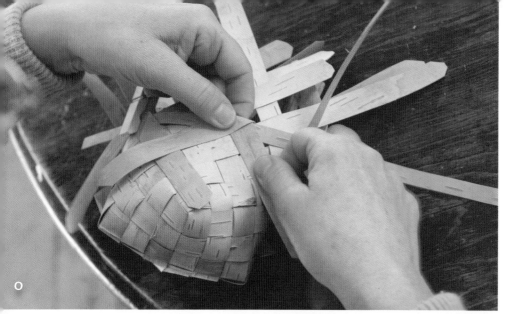

5. Take the extra strip set aside for the rim and cu[t] it in half lengthwise. Tuck under the corners th[at] have been folded down. Overlap the added strip on itself about 1", tuck the strip under, and make it snug by replacing the clothespins to hold it all in place (O–P). You are beginning to create the rim.

6. Continue to fold down the remaining edge strips. Hold them in place with clothespins. Fo[ld] just as you did with the previous corners. The slant should follow the previous weaving (Q–[R])

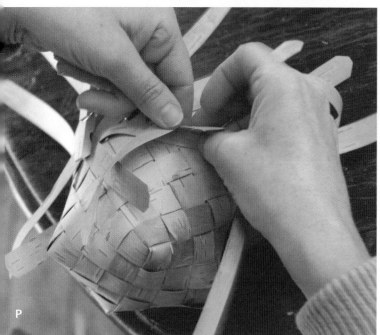

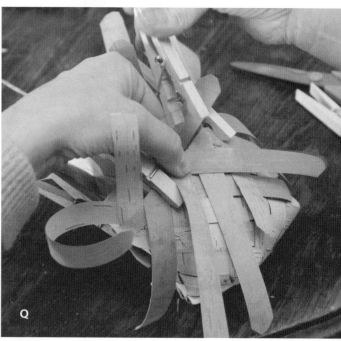

7. Check along the edge of the newly established rim to make sure that the strips continue to follow the over-and-under pattern. If some of the strips have come loose, reweave them (S).

8. The rest of the project will be weaving the strips back down over the previous weaving. Fold and tuck over the existing rim strips, using a fid when necessary (T–U). Continue to do this around the edge of the basket; you will tuck twelve times around the rim (V–X). Examine your basket and look for any gaps. If there are any, use your extra unused strips to fill in those gaps, being careful to hide the ends under the weaving (Y–Z). Trim off any excess (AA).

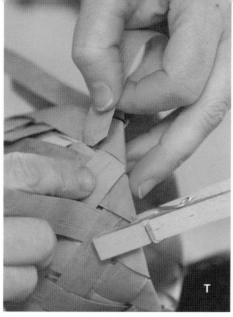

T

U

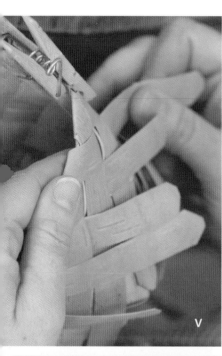

V

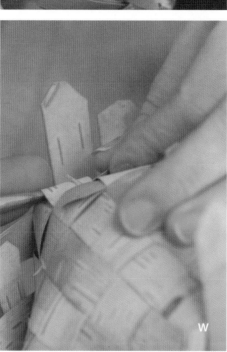

W

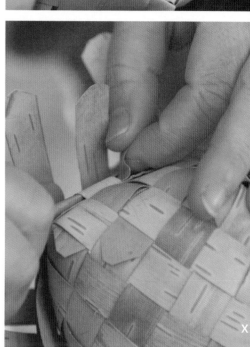

X

Y

Z

AA

# The Birch Bark Mile:
# SHOES

## JOHN ZASADA

Birch bark shoes were part of the historic birch tree culture in Scandinavia and Russia; according to legend, one could walk a "birch bark mile" (about 9½ miles) before wearing through the bottoms. Knowledge of weaving birch bark shoes traveled with Finnish and Swedish immigrants to Minnesota, where John Zasada has resurrected the art. Although he is not likely to "walk the mile" any time soon, he heartily enjoys creating bark footwear. As he weaves, he reflects upon the skilled hands that wove the first birch bark shoe. Through the ages, those hands guide his as he creates each wearable birch wonder.

## Materials

◆ 20 strips of birch bark, 1" wide x 12" long
◆ Several extra strips of birch bark, 1" wide x 12" long
◆ Several clothespins
◆ Scissors

1. Begin weaving three of the 1"-wide x 12"-long strips with the butter-colored side up. This color is what will eventually show on the exterior of the shoe. Add a fifth strip as the weaving progresses and use clothespins to secure the corners (**A–B**).

2. Fold the edges up to make a square (**C**).

3. Fold one strip in half and weave it standing upright inside of the square facing toward you (**D–E**). Turn the corner and trim the edge with scissors.

4. Weave in another strip to basket weave above the last piece, then around the corner (**F–G**). Trim. This is the toe of the shoe.

5. Bring the inner corner top strip up and over to the right and crease or fold to form a box over this created toe. Keep the weave just as tight (**H**).

6. Bring all bottom strips up and over, weaving in and out, to parallel and reflect the initial bottom surface. The bottom strips end up as a parallel "roof" to the bottom surface of the shoe (**I–J**).

**B**

**C**

**D**

**E**

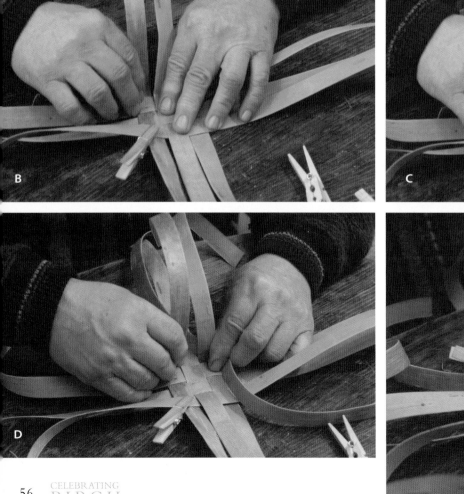

7. Pictures **D–F** show what will be the bottom of the shoe; **H** and **I** show the top of the toe. Turn over the toe of the shoe. You will see a three-strip-by-three-strip "diamond" pattern created by the weave. This looks the same as the top so you might want to place a mark on the outside surface of the top or bottom to keep track of where you are working. With the diamond representing the tip of the shoe closest to you, weave the third strip up (this requires bending the strip to an approximately 90 degree angle) in the over and under pattern, going through the two vertical strips and the two strips on the top of the shoe. Don't weave into the two crossing strips at the top of the diamond on the top of the shoe. This and subsequent strips woven from the shoe bottom into the top of the shoe will be parallel to the strips that form the side of the toe. The strips from the top and side of the toe are woven over and under, with the strips coming from the bottom of the shoe. When the weaving of the toe bottom strips to the top and toe top and side strips to the bottom is completed, the shoe will look like **K** and **L** from the top. A top view of what will be the inside of the shoe bottom is shown in **U**. The strips that you see making up the bottom are the strips that were the top of the toe and the two vertical strips as seen in **H** and **I**.

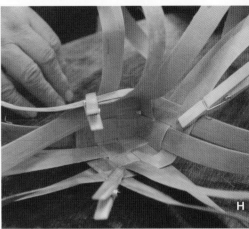

G

F

H

I

J

57

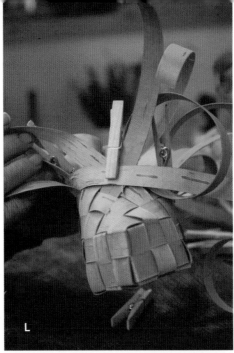

L

M

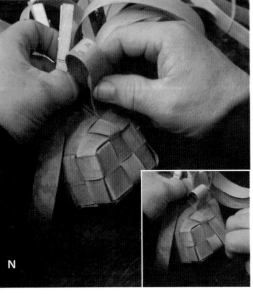

N

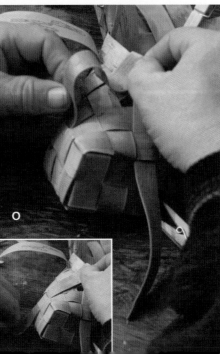

O

P

8. Take a new strip and add it to the two center strips (one coming from the right and one from the left) as in **K** and **L** by folding the center strips over the added piece. Weave the two strips into the shoe as shown in **N** and **O**. Note in **O** that you skip the first possible "under" weave and go to the second—this will be "corrected" as you progress in making the shoe. The piece that was added is woven over and under through the loose ends and toward what will be the heel of the shoe and it becomes a part of the bottom of the shoe—this is the strip seen in **U** as the strip furthest away from the toe in the bottom of the shoe.

9. To complete the construction of the "lip" that was created by addition of the strip in Step 8, two short pieces must be added. These pieces need to be long enough to cover the two pieces that were turned down in Step 8 (see **L** and **M**) and the two pieces on each side of this turned-down pair. **U** shows the turned-down pieces and the two strips on each side (my thumb is over the second strip to the right of the folded-down pair) after the strips have been added and the two strips to either side have been turned down and woven into the shoe. The first of these additional strips is added under one of the folded-down strips (**P** and **U**) and over both strips to either side (**P**). Next, the strip that was under the added strip in **L** and shown as the strip next to the strip under the left thumb in **U** is folded down and woven under the first strip where under-weaving is possible (**Q–S**). The same is done on the other side of the shoe. When the second strip is added, it will cover the strip that you just turned down. The second of the two strips on each side is folded over the added strip and woven under the strip just below the new strip (**T** and **U**).  Note that each of these turned-down strips has been turned over two strips. **U** and **V** show this, but you must look closely.

K

10. The next phase of shoe building will create the heel and build up the sides of the shoe from the shoe bottom. Again, refer to **U**, which shows the bottom of the shoe. The "loose ends" that come out from the bottom will form the heel and sides of the shoe.

**Splicing** will become essential at this point. Splicing is simply adding to a piece that is not long enough to continue the weave. It consists of adding in a piece by slipping it inside the strip that was too short and weaving it back under at least two crossing pieces (**V** shows a piece being spliced over the shorter piece and **X** shows an example of a completed splice). It is always better to splice well before making any turns or folds in your weaving, as these can be problem areas in maintaining a tight weave in any basketry project.

11. To form the heel, strips have to be folded up 90 degrees and then woven back toward the front of the shoe. Refer to **V**—the folding takes place in the strips shown at the tip of the clothespin under my right hand. When the folding is completed, the heel will look like **X**. The strips that form the heel are now woven into the strips toward the front and coming from of the bottom of the shoe. Each strip that is woven forward will be matched up with a strip coming from the bottom of the shoe. There will be pairs of strips woven down into the body of the shoe; each pair should be secured with a clothespin (**W**). The pairing is shown in **AA**. Each pair should have a strip coming together from two directions with one under its partner. An example of a pair is shown near the thumb in **X**.

Q

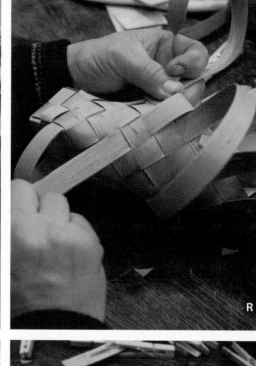

R

S

T

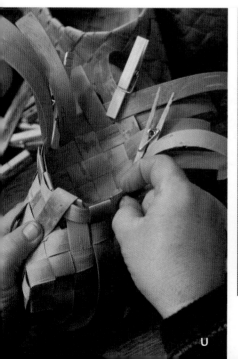

U

V

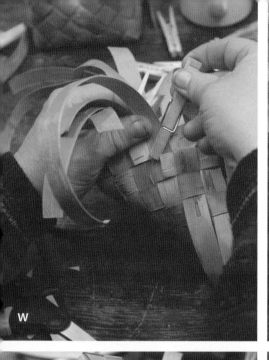

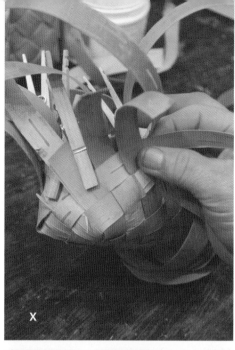

12. There are several ways to finish the top of the shoe. What is shown here is the "picket fence" top. The finish on the basket top shown on page 53 is another possibility. To make an individual "picket" from a pair of strips, fold a strip that is under its partner over that partner; when folded, its length will lie over itself. The other member of the pair is folded over its partner and will lie on top of itself when the fold is completed (Y–Z). Also see F and G on page 65 for an example of a completed "picket." Once the folds are completed, each strip is woven into the shoe body (BB–II). Continue around the top of the shoe until each pair is folded and woven into the shoe (FF and II). Each strip is woven entirely into the shoe; if it is too short to complete the weave, splice a piece in and continue. Each strip will eventually meet a strip

W

X

Y

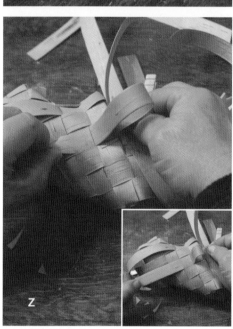

Z

AA

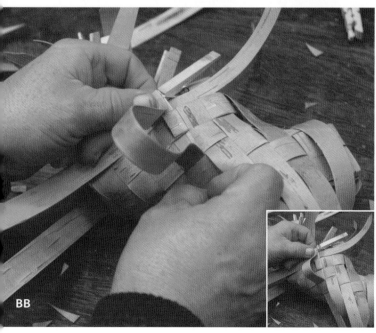

BB

CC

coming from the other direction—these strips should overlap one or two squares. When all of the strips have been woven in, the shoe will be about four layers of bark thick. This is the "double-weave" that is standard procedure in Scandinavian basketry—also shown for the basket and knife sheath.

3. A finished shoe is shown in **JJ**—this shoe is slightly larger than the shoe made with the above directions and using the three-by-three strip start (**A–C**). The dimensions of the shoe made with these instructions is about 7" from heel to toe and 3" wide. The height of the shoe at the heel is about 2". Other sizes can be made by varying the number of strips and the width of the strip.

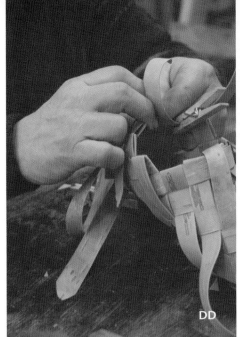

DD

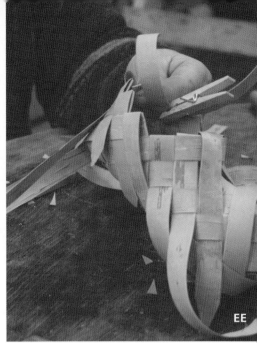

EE

FF

GG

HH

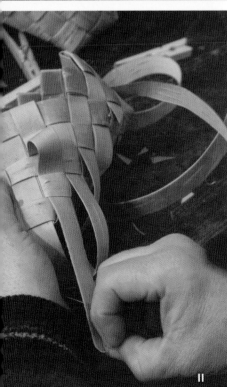

II

JJ

# *Butter-Colored Beauties:*
# KNIFE SHEATH

## JOHN ZASADA

A knife sheath is just as important as the tool it protects. Birch bark makes a sturdy and beautiful protective layer for any size or style of knife. These butter-colored beauties are a common sight on North House instructors' belts.

## Materials

- ◆ 5 or 6 strips of birch bark, 1" wide x 12" long
- ◆ Scissors
- ◆ Several clothespins
- ◆ Two thin pieces of wood
- ◆ Carving knife

1. Start by folding four strips of the 1"-wide x 12"-long birch bark; fold each in half (**A**). Tuck two together at this folded seam. Fold in the third and fourth strips, alternating with the beginning strips to make a diamond over-and-under pattern (**B**). This diamond is called the "gate."

2. Weaving from the gate, pull back and fold under the tail strip at a diagonal, then over and under (**C**). Do the same on the back side.

3. Work your way up the sheath, continually following the gate and using the outside strips.

4. After weaving to the top of the sheath, cross the strips, bevel the ends with scissors, and clip with clothespins (**D**). Next, weave back down the sheath to create a "double woven knife basket." The first step in back-weaving is to create pairs of strips—in this sheath that started with four strips there will be four pairs of strips. Secure each pair with a clothespin (**E**).

5. Finish with the picket fence top. In each pair that has been created, the strip that is under its partner is folded down over the partner to lie over itself when the fold is complete. The other member of the pair is also folded over and lies over itself when the fold is complete (**F**).

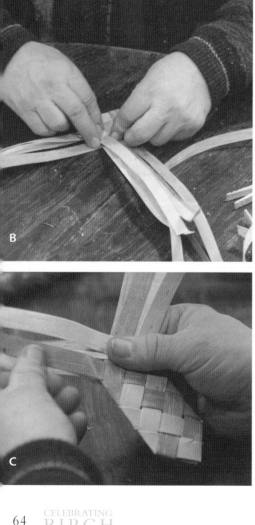

B

C

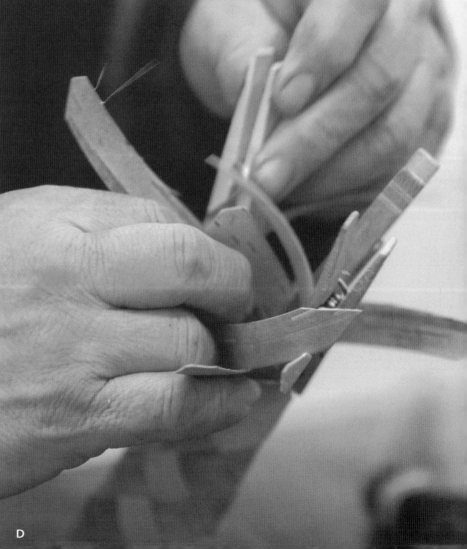

D

6. Once you have worked your way around the entire circle, weave the ends down farther in the sheath. Trim off any excess strip ends (G).

7. Weave in an extra strip over the top of any strip that has ended in your sheath partway, making sure to weave in over at least two diamonds (H). Splicing adds strength and continuity of color. Trim again after splicing.

8. When the sheath is completed, the next step is to make a protective wooden blade guard that slips inside the sheath. To make this guard, use two thin pieces of wood. Trace the blade shape on one of the pieces of wood and carve the wood out so that the blade fits and is level with the surface of the wood. The second piece of wood is fit over the piece that has been carved out. Wrap the two pieces of wood together and insert into the sheath. It may take several "fittings" to have the blade guard positioned just right—but with trial and error it should work.

**One final note:** This basic method of weaving can be used to make larger sheaths or wall baskets by increasing the number or width of the strips used in making the basket. This method can even be used to create a necktie!

E

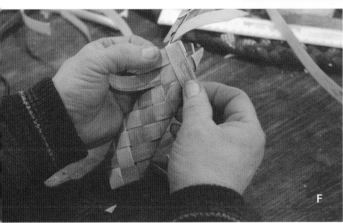

F

G

H

# Replacement for Scissors:
# BIRCH-BARK-HANDLED KNIFE

## MIKE SCHELMESKE

Birch bark makes a lovely, practical handle for a knife—it's amazingly durable, warm to the touch, and light. The bark will not slip in greasy, oily, or soapy hands and does not absorb water. If your knife handle starts to dull, lightly sand it with fine sandpaper and then rub it with oil.

Mike Schelmeske has been making knives since high school, and he uses his knife every day. It stays with him for carving spoons and bowls, whittling, trimming canoe paddles, sharpening pencils . . . it's his replacement for scissors.

When handling the blade, use great care to protect your fingers—wear cut-proof gloves or put plenty of painter's tape on the blade.

## Materials

- 8 squares of birch bark, roughly 1¼" x 1¼"
- Leather punch
- Knife
- Knife blade
- Propane torch
- 2 small pieces of reindeer antler
- Small block of birch burl
- Drill press
- Drill bit of same thickness as knife tang
- Tang rasp (like a mini keyhole saw) of same thickness as knife blade (see **P** on page 69)
- Pencil
- 2 washers
- Epoxy
- Clamp (see **S** on page 70)
- Blue painter's tape
- 4" vise
- Knife washer
- 8" mill bastard file
- Small ball-peen hammer
- Band saw or coping saw
- Four-in-one rasp
- 80- to 300-grit sandpaper (in 20-grit increments)
- Boiled linseed oil or linseed-turpentine mix

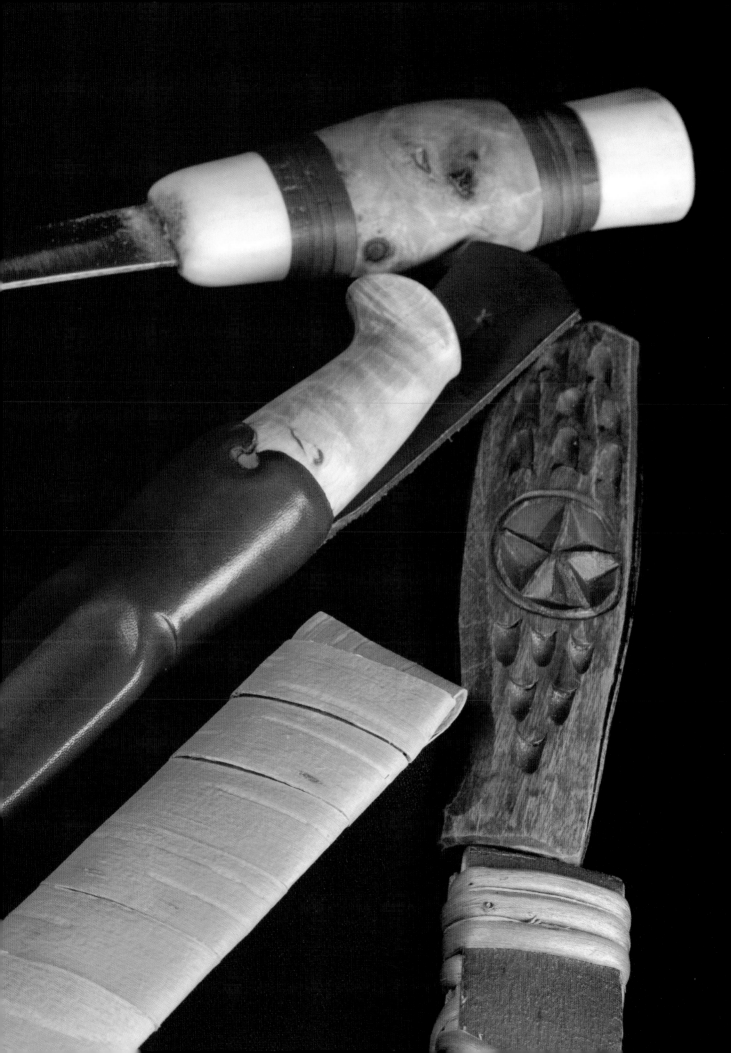

1. Use a leather punch to press holes in the center of eight 1¼" x 1¼" birch bark squares (A). Widen the holes with a knife and trim the squares with the knife as needed (B–C). Also, use a propane torch to heat and soften the last 1" of knife blade tang (the part to be inserted in the handle). Hold the tang pointed up when heating it to protect the temper of the blade. Soften it until the metal turns blue, making certain the tang lines up straight with the blade (D).

2. Lay out the squares of birch bark, knife blade, antler pieces, and small block of birch burl and measure them against the tang of the blade. Size the materials to a length slightly shorter than the overall length of the knife blade's tang (E–F).

3. Drill a hole in one antler piece with a bit that is of equal thickness to the knife blade's tang. Following with a tang rasp, bore this hole to the taper of the tang, filing down as you work. Clean down level to a place where the blade can fit snugly up against the stacked pieces (G–I).

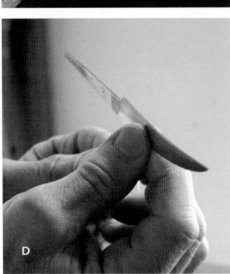

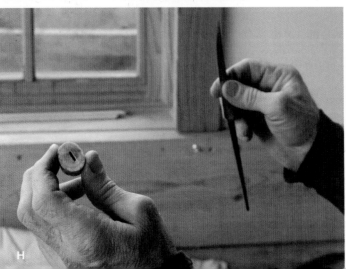

4. Place a pencil mark on the antler piece on each side of the blade and rasp down the hole in the antler piece at a 45-degree angle to these marks, creating a resting spot for the blade (J–L).

5. Next, find the center of the birch burl block and drill a hole through it using the same bit as in Step 3. After drilling, rasp just as in Step 3 (M–N).

6. Fit the birch burl block to the blade and stack birch bark pieces on either side to balance. Repeat Step 3 on the additional antler piece (O–P).

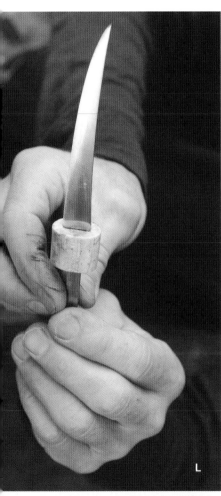

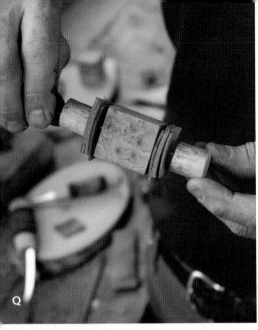

Q

R

7. Epoxy the first half of the stack together: one antler piece (placed closest to the blade), four birch bark squares, and the birch burl block. Clamp the stack and let it dry. After the epoxy has dried, add the remaining birch bark squares and antler piece, epoxying them in place. Clamp and let dry (Q–S).

8. Using painter's tape to protect the blade, place the handle into the vise and fit the washer on the end of the handle. To do this, cut a groove with a file approximately ⅛" above where the washer will lie and snap the tang off. File the remaining end of the tang until it is ¹⁄₁₆" above the washer. Using a ball-peen hammer, lightly tap the end of the tang, mushrooming it out to cover and pull the washer down toward the knife blade (T–W).

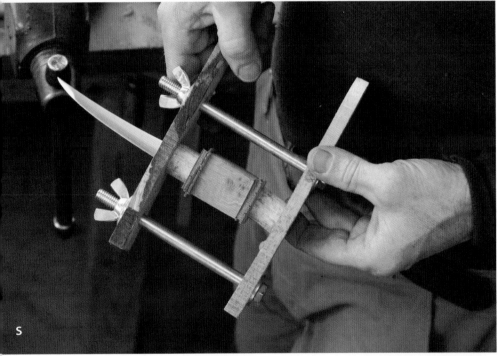

S

T

U

V

W

9. Next, use the pencil to trace profiles of the knife handle shape. In order to have a comfortable grip, it should be fuller in the center. Also trace the top profile (X–Y).

10. Using a band saw or a coping saw, roughly cut out the side and top profiles, removing as much material as possible while preserving the traced profile lines (Z–AA).

11. Use a four-in-one rasp to shape the handle, working from both ends in toward the center. Work as close to the pencil lines as possible to taper away from the barrel shape. File with each side of the rasp, finishing with the finest (BB).

12. After filing, switch to sandpaper and sand the handle, starting with 80-grit and working up to 300-grit in 20-grit increments. Sand out all scratches. After sanding, lightly dampen the handle to raise inconsistencies in the grain. Sand to smooth. Finish the handle with linseed oil or a linseed-turpentine mix (CC).

X

Y

Z

AA

BB

CC

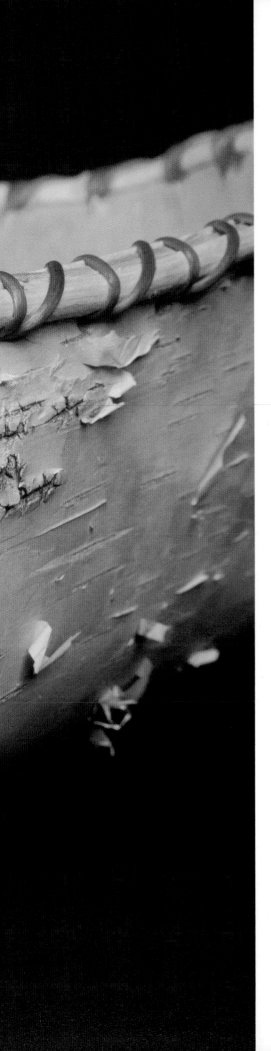

# BIRCH
## LORE AND
## LEGENDS

"YOU SEE, THE BIRCH, WHICH GROWS ABOUT AS
OLD AS A HUMAN BEING, IS REALLY THE MOST
MAGICAL AND BEAUTIFUL OF ALL TREES . . ."
—*Lise Lunge-Larsen, folklorist and storyteller*

Because the birch met so many practical needs,
it is no surprise that the tree soon found itself a
place in the lore of many cultures of the world.
From poetry and literature to history and myth,
we'll take a look at birch's place and significance
throughout the ages.

# THE LORE OF BIRCH

## LISE LUNGE-LARSEN

The birch was the first tree to colonize Europe and North America after the last ice age. It acts as a "nurse tree" by offering protection to other, slower-growing trees, and its small leaves cast only a little shadow, allowing other plants to easily grow beneath it. Perhaps it is these qualities, along with its graceful, feminine shape, that have made the birch a symbol of rebirth and renewal. Birch also provides for many practical needs, which may be the reason that the American Forestry Association, in 1920, chose the birch as its first Mother Tree of America.

*left*
*The Bench.* Birch bark collage. Dominique Leroy Prince, Minnesota, 2006.

*right*
*Birch Stand—Spring* (batik). Gail Hedstrom, Minnesota, 2005.

# TRADITIONS AND SYMBOLS OF BIRCH

The birch has been important to people wherever it grows, and there are countless traditions and stories connected to it. In Scandinavian mythology, the birch is consecrated to Thor, the god of thunder. Thor is the strongest of all the gods, but because thunderstorms occur most often in spring and because the rain makes everything grow, Thor is also associated with fertility and rebirth. Since birch is Thor's tree, it was thought to have many protective qualities, and a birch branch attached to a house would protect the occupants from all kinds of trouble, especially lightning, the evil eye, gout, and barrenness.

In Celtic lore, the birch holds a similarly high position. The ancient Irish Tree Alphabet begins with the letter B (beth), which means "birch." Birch is also a symbol of new beginnings and a symbol of young love. In Wales, for example, a girl would give her sweetheart a piece of birch as a love token. The gift was a sign that the young man could begin his courtship.

*eft*
*Birch Stand—Summer* (batik). Gail Hedstrom, Minnesota, 2005.

*right*
*The Immigrant.* Birch bark collage. Dominique Leroy Prince, Minnesota, 2006.

In ancient Rome, by contrast, the birch was a symbol of power and authority. Birch branches were tied around an ax with the blade sticking out. These rather threatening bouquets were called *fasces* and were carried ahead of Roman processions to let the people know that dignitaries were coming. It is from these fasces that we get the word *fascist*.

In ancient times, bad behavior and even mental disorders were thought to be caused by malevolent spirits that had gotten inside people. Birch was believed to have the power to drive out evil, and for this reason, switches made from birch branches were used to beat the evil spirits out of lunatics. Schoolmasters have used birch switches on unruly students since ancient times, and to receive a "birching" means to receive a good thrashing. Also, sweeping the house with a "besom broom," a broom made of birch, was the best way to get rid of a witch.

Indeed, birch brooms are a rich source of tradition. Witches were thought to ride them. In Norway, a hag, the personification of the Black Death, might carry one. If she appeared dragging a birch broom, the village would be swept clean and everyone would die. If she appeared with a rake, some would be spared. In Newfoundland, it was thought to be unlucky to make birch brooms in May, for they would sweep the family away. On a more pleasant note, birch brooms were used in Scotland to sweep the ice in the ancient game of curling.

The birch tree has also played an important part in many of the oldest annual celebrations: It was the traditional yule log that was burned during the midwinter ceremonies to drive out the spirit of the old year and welcome the new. A birch trunk was also traditionally used as a maypole because of its association with springtime, fertility, and birth. And when a new baby was born, it was best to place the infant in a cradle made from birch.

The stories about birch are many. The English believed that the birch was the Tree of Paradise. To Estonians, the birch is the personification of their country. Norwegians and Swedes say that the dwarf birch was once a full-grown tree, but when its rods were used to whip Christ during His Passion, the tree became so ashamed that it shrank and crawled northward to hide. It has been hiding its stunted head ever since, never growing taller than two feet.

In Finnish folklore, the first birch is said to have sprung from a maiden's tear, and the Finnish creation epic, the *Kalevala*, tells how the hero,

*far left*
*Birch Stand—Fall* (batik). Gail Hedstrom, Minnesota, 2005.

*left*
Birch twig broom.

©iStockphoto.com/jennyhome

79

Väinämöinen, made his harp from a birch, with strings from the hair of a singing maiden. When he played on his harp, "the mountains sounded out like organs, all the crags rang out, stumps on the heaths jumped, rocks on the shores cracked, and the leaves took to frolicking."

In the Russian version of Cinderella, a birch tree functions as the Fairy Godmother. It grows on the spot where the cinder girl's mother lies buried. Branches from this wonderful birch help the girl magically perform the impossible tasks that her stepmother gives her. It even produces the clothes and horses she needs to get to the ball and win her prince.

In Siberian folklore, the birch is the tree of life. In the far north, they say, grows an enormous birch. Its leaves are as big as bear paws and its catkins as long as whips. At the foot of this birch is a well that is the source of the water of life. If you dip a cup made of birch into this well and drink its water, you will have eternal life.

*left*
Lathe-turned birch bowl. Bob Carls, Minnesota, 2006.

*right*
*Birch Stand—Winter* (batik). Gail Hedstrom, Minnesota, 2005.

# THE BIRCH FAIRY

*Lise Lunge-Larsen*

For her retelling of this fairy tale, Lise Lunge-Larsen was inspired by two different versions of the story. One is "The Wood Fairy," told by Virginia Haviland in her book *Favorite Fairy Tales Told in Czechoslovakia* (Little Brown, 1959). The other is "The Wild Woman of the Birch Wood," told by Anne Pellowski in her book *Hidden Stories in Plants* (Simon & Schuster Children's Publishing, 1990).

Once upon a time, there was a little girl named Betushka who lived with her mother in a birch forest. Betushka's mother was a poor widow who owned almost nothing except her little cottage, two goats, and a spindle for spinning thread. But despite their poverty, Betushka was a happy child who always had a song on her lips and a dance in her steps.

Every day from spring until fall, Betushka took the goats out to pasture in a grove in the birch forest. She brought her lunch, a bundle of flax, and the spindle. All morning she sang while she spun, and at lunch she shared her bread with the goats and picked berries for dessert. After lunch, she got up and danced among the birches, for Betushka loved nothing better than to dance. But she never forgot to look after the goats or to finish her spinning, for when she came home, her mother would expect the spindle full of thread to sell at market.

One spring day when Betushka was getting ready to dance, a beautiful lady suddenly appeared. She wore a white gossamer dress that floated about her. A wreath of birch branches crowned her lovely golden hair.

"Do you like to dance?" asked the lady in a sweet voice.

"Oh, I love nothing better!" exclaimed Betushka. "I would dance all day if I didn't have to finish my spinning."

"May I dance with you a little?" asked the lady. Betushka nodded, and when the lady took her hands, the birds began to sing the most beautiful songs. Betushka and the lovely lady twirled and spun around, their steps so light that hardly a blade of grass bent under their feet. Betushka forgot all about her goats and the spinning as she danced to the music of the birds. She and the lady danced all afternoon until the sun was about to go down. Then, all at once, the lady vanished and Betushka was left alone in the birch grove. Luckily, the goats had not strayed, but the spindle was only half full.

She hurried home, and when her mother asked for the spindle, she pretended to have left it behind in the woods. "I'll spin more tomorrow," she told herself. She did not mention the lady.

The next day the beautiful lady appeared again, saying, "Betushka, let us dance."

"I can't dance until I have filled my spindle with thread, or my mother will be angry with me," exclaimed Betushka.

"If you will dance with me now, I will do the spinning for you," said the lady. At once, the birds began their song, and Betushka and the lady danced. This time, they stopped before sunset, and the lady twined the bundle of flax around a slender birch. In no time at all, the spindle was filled with thread, and Betushka ran home happily.

The next day the same thing happened. Betushka and the lady danced, and when they finished, the lady said, "Dancing with you has made me very happy, and I have a little present to thank you." She handed Betushka a silvery white bag that was beautifully embroidered with designs of leaves and catkins.

"Do not look inside the bag before you are home," the lady warned. Betushka promised she would not and gave the lady a hug. "Don't forget this," the lady added and handed her the spindle. To Betushka's dismay, the spindle was only half full. Again she had forgotten to finish her spinning. She almost felt like crying, but the lovely lady laughed when she saw her face. She tapped the spindle three times and, all at once, it was filled with beautiful silvery thread. "Now your mother won't be angry with you," said the lady.

Betushka thanked her over and over, and then she set off for home. But after a little while, she became very curious about the bag and thought, "Surely I can take just a little peek?" She untied the string and looked inside.

But all she could see were dried old birch leaves. She dug inside the bag but could find nothing else. In disappointment, she threw a handful of leaves on the ground and was about to pour out the rest when she realized that the leaves would make excellent bedding for her goats.

At home, her mother stood in the door waiting, and Betushka handed her the spindle. Looking at the silvery white thread in wonder, Betushka's mother exclaimed, "How did you come by this marvelous thread? Surely you did not spin this yourself."

Then Betushka told her mother everything about the lady and the dancing.

"That must have been the Birch Fairy," said Betushka's mother, amazed. "She rarely shows herself and only to those she favors. Did she give you anything? The Birch Fairy is famous for her generosity to those who please her."

"She gave me this bag, but there's only dry birch leaves inside," said Betushka, and she opened the bag. But this time, there were no dried leaves. Instead, the bag was filled with shining gold coins.

Oh, how Betushka wished she had not looked and tossed out so many leaves. She and her mother ran into the woods looking for the tossed leaves, but they never found them. Still, with the gold and the money the silver thread fetched at the market, Betushka's mother was able to buy a small farm and some cows. Betushka had lovely dresses to wear when she went outside, and even though she no longer had to tend the goats, she often went into the forest to look for the Birch Fairy, but she never saw her again.

*Summer Birch* (mosaic).
Nancy Seaton, Minnesota, 2005.

83

## A PRACTICAL SIDE OF BIRCH

Paper birch was and is arguably the most versatile tree species in the northern forest. One or two parts of commonly associated trees may have been used by indigenous peoples and may still be used today; but as for paper birch and the white-barked birches, every part of the tree has been used in one or more of the cultures where these species occur.

The nomadic people who live in the northernmost parts of Russia and Scandinavia greatly esteemed birch. For them, it was the source of many items: from shoes and clothing to roof coverings and light. Because birch burns so well, it also makes excellent torches. One legend tells how the evil Tsjudes want to kill the Saami people and take their land. They force an old Saami man to guide them to the village where the Saami have gathered. One night, the guide leads them over a mountain. The Tsjudes ski tied to each other so they won't get lost in the dark. The guide brings them to a sheer cliff and then throws a birch torch over the cliff shouting, "Follow me!" The torch continues to burn brightly as it falls down, and the Tsjudes set off after it, thinking the guide is skiing downhill. They are all killed in the fall; the Saami people are saved by birch's ability to burn strongly.

*below*
(Left to right)
Antler-tipped ski pole with deerskin handle, balsam shaft and red-osier dogwood basket. Church skis, Telemark style. Two pairs of Saami-style skis. Mark Hansen, Minnesota, 2006.

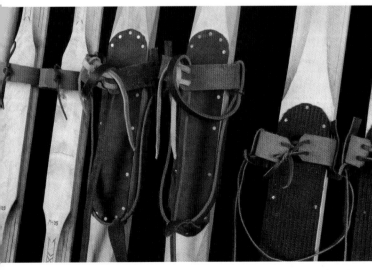

*above*
Birch ski binding variations with both traditional and contemporary materials. Mark Hansen, Minnesota, 2006.

# LANGUAGE

*Joanne Hart*

From *Witch Tree: A Collaboration* (Holy Cow Press, 1992).

Joanne Hart makes her home among
the Grand Portage Anishnabeg in
northeastern Minnesota. She writes poetry
to acknowledge the respect for life that
she is so often taught to recognize there.

What carries culture is the sound
old women breathe in winter time—
stories in grandmother tongue
that rustle from behind the doors,
settle into corners where
firelight can color them.

The way the grandmothers describe
is how the breath of tribes reflects
light from everything that is—
morning mist over the lake,
ropes of chimney smoke that hang
cabins from an evening sky.

Shapes of sound from palate, teeth,
susurration and the sharp
staccato, the rise and fall
grandmothers use to decorate
the story telling, pattern the mind
the way templates from newspaper

or birchbark—stars, the new moon, leaves,
blossoms—pattern their basketry.
Tribal people recognize
how stories come from the elders
shape intact, but each retelling
unique, alive. The grandmothers

say when someone goes into
the woods and later tells of it,
Anishinabe words describe
each little leaf and twig. The telling
carries back the place, they say.
The words will always keep the place.

*above*
*Floral Motif.* Etched
winter bark. Eric Mase,
Minnesota, 2005.

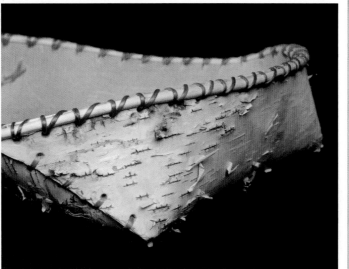

*left*
Nooskochinaagan wild rice
winnowing tray. Erik Simula,
Minnesota, 2005.

Many indigenous North American cultures also hold the birch in high esteem, using it to fashion utensils, birch bark trays, baskets, storage boxes, maple sugar cones, pots to boil water (which are reinforced with spruce gum), dishes, cups, and, of course, birch bark canoes. Because birch bark resists rotting and repels water, Native Americans have historically used it to waterproof their dwellings. According to some traditional Ojibwe stories, birch received these qualities as a reward for having sheltered Nanabozho, the trickster god, from the thunderbirds. It was the angry thunderbirds' wings that gave the birch its distinctive markings (see "Nanabozho" on page 88). Interestingly, according to other stories, the birch actually received its markings as a punishment for refusing to obey its Maker!

Because it is waterproof and will not easily rot, birch bark was useful as a form of paper. The Ojibwe Midewiwin scrolls depicting history, stories, and sacred teachings were made of etched birch bark. Ojibwe artist Norval Morriseau's early works pay homage to the Midewiwin scrolls. Thomas Jefferson wrote to Lewis and Clark as they were about to leave on their expedition that they should keep daily records on "paper of birch, as less liable to injury from damp than common paper." And in Russia, birch bark was often preferred for keeping important family records because of its durability. As noted earlier, many centuries-old birch bark scrolls, still quite legible, still exist.

So you see, the birch, which grows about as old as a human being, is really the most magical and beautiful of all trees. Without it, our lives would be poor indeed.

*right*
Various styles of birch containers. Left to right: Canoe basket with interior bark exposed, bound with spruce root. Berry basket with Saami motif and woven Northern white cedar inner bark handle. Scandinavian-style cylindrical container with black ash burl lid. Large birch bark container with hand carved cherry lid and handles. Dennis Chilcote, Minnesota, 2006.

*left*
floral motif etched in
winter birch bark. Eric Mase,
Minnesota, 2006.

*above*
Birch bark canoe.
Eric Mase, Minnesota, 2006.

*right*
inside view of above canoe,
featuring cedar ribs, birch
thwart, and leather tumpline.
Eric Mase, Minnesota, 2006.

# NANABOZHO

**Traditional Ojibwe Story**
*Courtesy of the Grand Portage Band
of Minnesota Chippewa*

The Grand Portage Band of Minnesota Chippewa—also
called Ojibwe and, traditionally, Anishnabeg—live on
Lake Superior. The land that North House Folk School
occupies was once theirs. They offer to share this story
with all people.

This is a traditional Anishnabeg story. We ask that in
keeping with Anishnabe customs, the story not be read
in late spring, summertime, or early fall. The Nanabozho
story can only be told when snow is on the ground and
the thunderbirds have gone south.

*right*
*Beary Babies* (acrylic and
ink on bark). Mac Squires,
Ontario, 2005.

*far right*
*Birch Clump* (acrylic and
ink on bark). Lloyd Scherer,
Minnesota, 2005.

*Abading gizhigak mewisha, Nanabozho babamoset
wedi nopiming. Ingodingo kaisha wabamat animikig
binesiwag. Apitchi nishkadisiway iniw animikig.
Ginishkinawawon Nanabozho.*

One day long ago, Nanabozho was walking in the woods.
All at once he saw some thunderbirds. They were angry
thunderbirds. They were angry at Nanabozho.

*Animikig gibisegowag wedi inakea Nanabozho. Gi
bashkamowok animikig, besho Nanabozho. Minawa dash,
minawa wasigan ongo binesiwag. Osam gi gijika Nanabozho.
Ogibanaowan Nanabozho apine, animikig.*

The thunderbirds began to fly at Nanabozho. Then they
began to shoot lightning bolts at Nanabozho. Again and again
the lightning bolts flew, but Nanabozho was too fast for them.
The lightning bolts missed Nanabozho every time.

*Nanabozho gi bimibato wedi maygwakab. Apitchi Nanabozho
gi madjibaiwet. Nanabozho kaisha wabamat chi wigwasimitig.
Mi dash ima bindig mitigong kaisha gwashgonet Nanabozho.*

Nanabozho ran quickly through the woods to get away from
the thunderbirds. Soon he saw a large birch tree. There was a
good place to hide in the tree. Into the tree he jumped.

*Winge mashkawadisi Nanabozho. Gawi ogi gashkitosinawa
chi baganawat aw mitigong. Geget chi nishkadisiwag ongo
animikig. Animikig obibetakgoshkawawon mitigon. Apan ogi
betakgoshkawawon a'aw mitig.*

Nanabozho had great powers. The lightning could not strike
the tree. This made the thunderbirds very angry. Crash! Crash!
The big birds crashed against the tree. Again and again they
crashed against the tree.

*Waibago ogimikawawon aw mitigong, Oningwiganon
ogi apitchiotonawa wi miganawad mitigon. Wewenisago
Nanabozho gikasa ima bindig mitigong. Geget mi kaisha
madjigibisegowag animikig.*

Soon there were marks on the tree. The marks
came from the crashing of the wings on the tree trunk.
But still Nanabozho was safe inside the tree. Finally,
the thunderbirds flew away. They were very, very angry.

*Apitchi nishkadisiwag animikig. Nanabozho gi bisagaam
mitigong. Migwitch! Migwitch gi bimadjieg ikito Nanabozho.
Nimikwendan apitchi gi minadodawe.*

Nanabozho came out from the tree. "Thank you! Thank you for saving me," he exclaimed. "I will remember how good you have been."

*Nanabozho chi nanagadawendang. In gikendan ikito Nanabozho, migo apane nimikwenanamon. Nebewa giga abijitonawa wigwas.*

Then Nanabozho thought and thought. "I know," he said, "I must remember you every day. We will find many uses for birch bark."

*Gi abijitonawa wigwas wigiwamiken minawa jimanensiken minawa kinego anoj. Kitchi gawin ogi bagitchigesiwiag a'aw wigwas mitigong minawa geabi eshinagwot a'aw mitigong.*

Today the birch bark is used in many ways. It is used for building wigwams and canoes and many other things. And for many years, lightning never struck a birch tree, and the birch trees still have the marks left by the angry thunderbirds.

*Mi'iw.*

The end.

Lloyd
Scherer

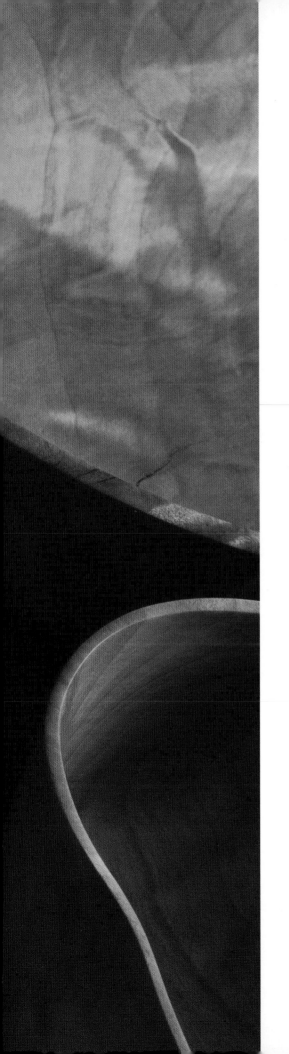

# BIRCH
# WOOD

"THERE IS MORE TO THE BIRCH TREE
THAN THE BARK ITSELF. AMONG ARTISTS AND
CRAFTSPEOPLE, BIRCH WOOD IS ALSO DESIRABLE."
—*John Zasada, forester and instructor*

While the use of birch bark has long been celebrated as an essential ingredient for traditional craft, the wood of the tree has also been utilized in a variety of ways. Often worked and carved "green," the wood's strength and beautiful grain are attributes that are both of value to traditional craft artisans. Burls and other types of character wood are also highly sought after.

# Three or Four a Night:
# SPOON

## MIKE SCHELMESKE

Mike Schelmeske's love of craft comes from making something that is beautiful and graceful as well as useful. One of his heroes of utilitarian craft is Penti Miller, a Finnish immigrant living in rural Brimson, Minnesota. Mike says, "Seeing Penti's spoons changed the look of my spoons from then on. Seeing his shop and tools and how he worked was great—he was so resourceful. He was using old tools that I had only seen previously in books." This straightforward way of passing on traditional knowledge from generation to generation is a big part of the vision at North House.

This spoon is best made with winter wood, as is dries whiter because the sap is down in the roots. Working next to the woodstove is another benefit of making spoons in the winter—the shavings go right into the stove. The pattern for the spoon is inspired by the work of Penti Miller.

### Materials

- Green birch log or wedge of birch
- Splitting maul
- Wooden spoon pattern
- Pencil
- Ax
- Knife
- Japanese pull saw
- 1" (25 mm) gouge
- Several sheets of newspaper
- Paper bag
- Sandpaper, from 60- to 220-grit
- Edible oil: mineral oil, flaxseed oil, boiled linseed oil, or olive oil

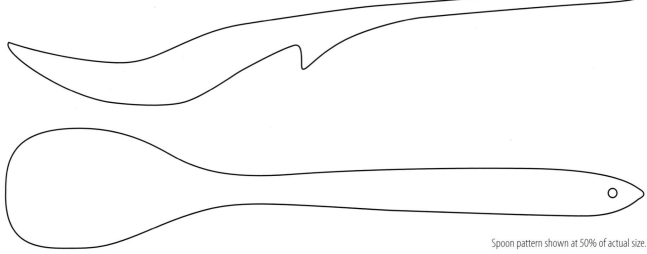

Spoon pattern shown at 50% of actual size.

A

B

1. Beginning with a birch log, use a splitting maul to split the log in half (A–C). Using a spoon pattern, lay out blanks on the end of the log with a pencil, much the way you would slice a pie (D). Wedge and split the log again (E).

2. Get rid of the heartwood with an ax (F).

E

C

D

F

3. Clear the bark side just enough to lay out the top profile of the spoon pattern (G–H). Trace this pattern on the bark side in order to show the concentric rings in the spoon's bowl. Center the spoon on the visible growth rings in the wood (I).

4. Square off this face with the ax until it is almost flush with the side of the spoon's bowl. Continue down the side, arriving at a parallel surface. Repeat on the opposite side (J–K).

5. Trace the side profile pattern of the spoon onto one side of the blank, placing the handle top flush with the top of the blank (L–M).

N

O

6. Chop away as much wood as possible, working from the bottom edge of the spoon. Work close to the traced lines, but not too close—leave some room for error and adjustment. The more wood you take off with the ax, the less you'll have to remove later on with a knife (N–O).

7. Draw a pencil line on the bottom side of the spoon, parallel with the spoon's hook. Make a stop cut with a Japanese pull saw, ¼" deep, following the side profile pattern as a guide (P).

8. From the bottom, chop in at an angle to meet the previous cut made in Step 7 (Q–R). Next, sheer off a bit more of the bowl's bottom (S).

9. With the ax, cut down into the bowl's top face to the pattern line, making a slight curve (T). Use lighter and more controlled chop strokes than before.

P

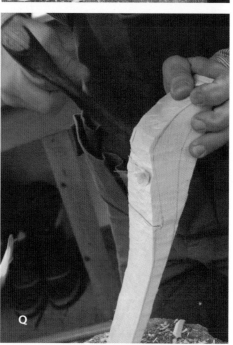

Q

R

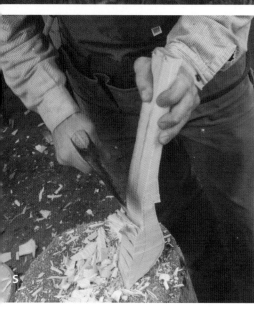

S

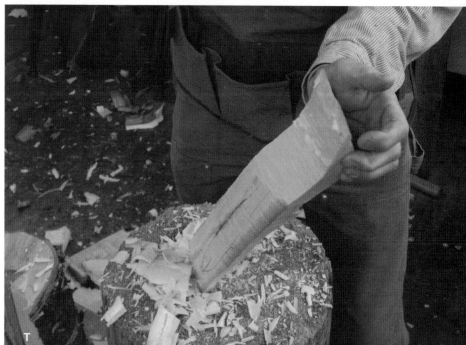

T

0. Retrace your top pattern, leaving marks where the bowl belongs (U).

1. Rough out the sides of the spoon with the ax, coming as close as possible to the previously traced line. Repeat on the other side (V–W).

2. Retrace any marks that have faded, and draw additional bowl lines inside the existing lines to create a lip. Also draw a line straight down the middle of the bowl from the hook. Use the ax to create a bevel on each side of this line, working your way back to the center of the hook. The rings should surround your centerline in concentric circles (X–Y).

3. Use a knife to trim up the front edge. Work from the corners to the center (Z).

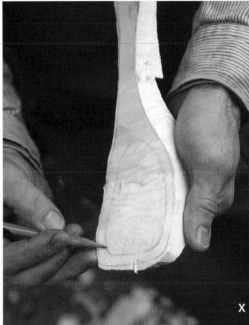

AA

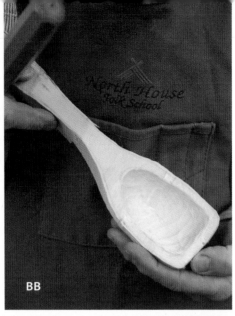

BB

14. Switch to a gouge to carve out the bowl, again working from the edges into the center. Choke up on the gouge, using your palm for adequate leverage and control. Carve a smooth curve along the inside of the bowl, making the thickness taper from the thin edges to ¾" where the bowl joins the handle (**AA–BB**).

15. Next, work the outside of the bowl. Use a knife to carve to the side line, making certain to work toward the hook from both sides. When carving, use your thumb and hand for leverage. Carve out the bowl as much as possible on all sides (**CC–EE**).

16. Carve a seat on the base of the spoon's bowl so it will rest carefully when it is set down (**FF–GG**).

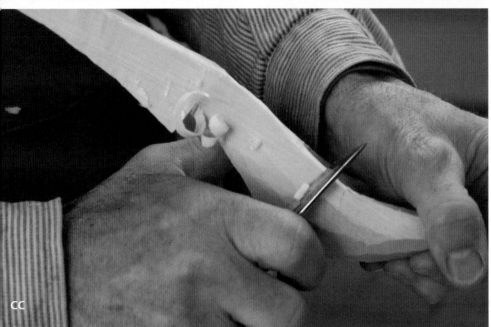

CC

DD

EE

FF

GG

17. Next, work the hook and handle down in the same manner as in Step 15. Finish with the end of the spoon (**HH–KK**).

18. When you are satisfied with your carving, wrap the spoon in a couple of layers of newspaper and dry it in a paper bag for two weeks. When the spoon is fully dry, make any final smoothing with the knife and then sand it with sandpaper, starting with 60-grit and moving up toward 220-grit. The handle and outside of the spoon may be left unsanded if you wish. Your spoon can be finished with mineral oil, flaxseed oil, boiled linseed oil, or even olive oil (**LL–MM**).

HH

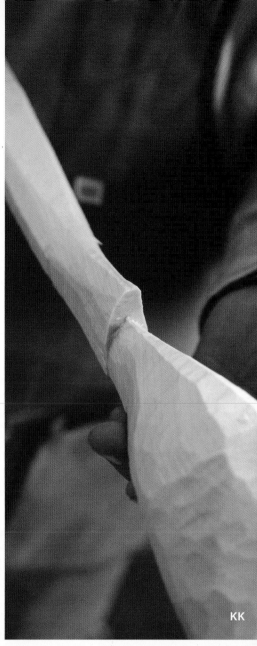

KK

II

JJ

LL

MM

# In the Arc of the Wrist:
# CARVED BOWL

## JON STROM

A bowl is one of the earliest utensils, but its service on a daily basis has never diminished. The opportunity to create an object that serves daily is very appealing. Discovering a tradition from the Swedish part of his heritage was too exciting for Jon Strom to resist. He learned to create a bowl with a design that emerges as the tools are used in the motion of the wrist's arc and are guided by the aesthetics of the eye. Bowls that can be chopped from a log, cut from a tree grown nearby, are wonderful things. If Jon can leave part of the tree's unique features in the bowl, such as heartwood color, figurative grain, or even some of the bark, the excitement climbs even higher. These factors are what enable him to create a truly individual piece each time he takes the blade to the log.

## Materials

- Freshly cut birch log, 16" long x 6" to 7" diameter
- Splitting wedges
- Mallet
- Small carving ax
- Vise or other hold-down device
- Pencil
- Bowl-carving adz
- Shallow gouge
- Medium-grit sandpaper (optional)
- Plane (optional)
- Olive oil or edible flaxseed oil

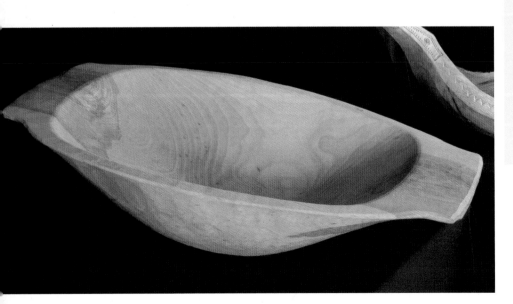

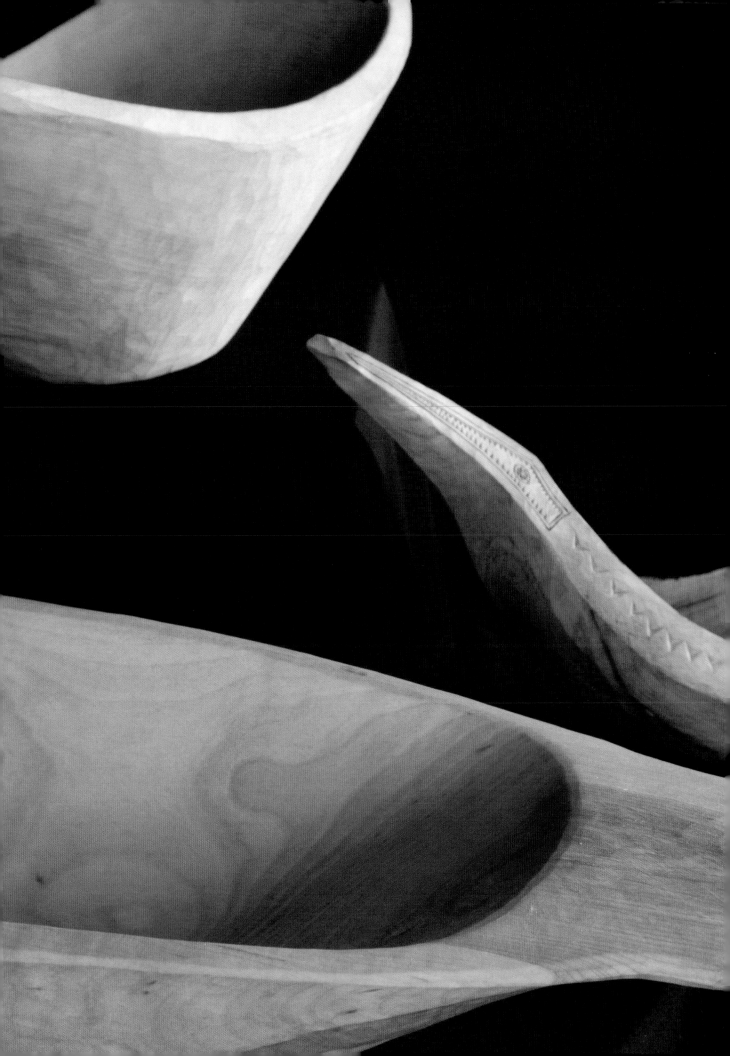

1. Select a freshly cut birch log or one that is still wet inside with the bark still intact. If the ends have dried, cut them off to avoid cracks in the bowl. Pieces from the lower trunk of a tree are usually clear of knots, and a log 16" long and 6" to 7" in diameter is a good size to begin with **(A)**.

2. Split the log in half through the pith using wedges and a mallet. Remember, the pith is not always in the direct center of the log or tree. Select a line that will give the most symmetrical shape to your bowl. After splitting, choose one half (preferably knot and blemish free) for your bowl **(B–C)**.

3. Pieces of birch with wide, dark red centers tend to dry and split at a different rate in the heartwood. If this center is visible in your log, chop most of this away with an ax. After chopping away the center, true this side to as flat a plane as possible **(D–E)**.

4. Choose one side of the log for the top of the bowl—the round side or the inner flat side. If you choose to have the inner flat side up, flatten a small area opposite it that will serve as the bottom of the bowl (F). Flatten an area about 3" wide along the length of the log with the ax. This flat bottom will sit down when wedged in a carving bench or on a workbench when using a vise. Clamp down or wedge the bowl's ends.

5. Use a pencil to trace an oval for the inside of the bowl. Mark a preliminary shape for the outside of the bowl as well. Leave ½" of wood on the sides and 2" to 3" on the ends for handles or finger grips (G–H).

6. Check that the stock is secure in the vise and begin chipping out small pieces with a bowl-carving adz (I–K).

F

G

H

I

J

K

103

L

7. Let the swing move with the adz and its arc. This swing will determine the smooth flow of the inside of the bowl. Strive to get a flat area in the bottom of the bowl, but avoid sharp corners where the ends and the sides flow into the bottom (L).

8. Check the depth occasionally and leave a ½" thickness in the bowl's bottom (M–N).

9. This is the time when the stock can be clamped most easily, so you'll want to smooth the inside as much as possible by shaving it with a shallow gouge. Aim to leave a slightly flat surface in the bottom, going right up to the line that was drawn (O–P).

M

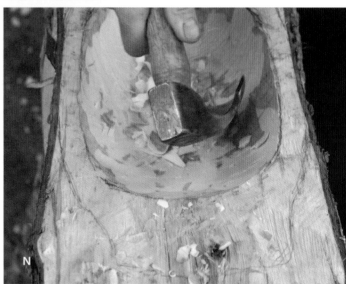

N

O

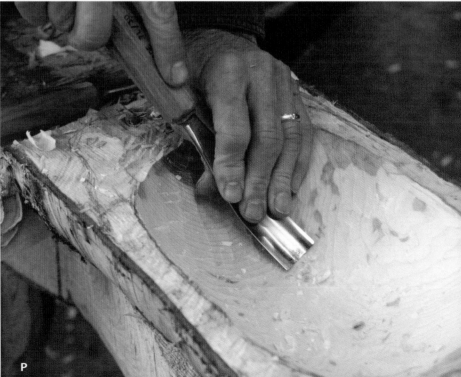

P

0. When you are satisfied with the inside, take the stock out of the holding device and trace the outside shape, leaving the ends progressively thicker where the grain is shorter; then, make a simple shape for handles or finger grips. Transfer the points from inside where the ends meet the bottom to the outside bottom, and mark these with a pencil. Also draw lines for the handle depth (**Q**).

1. Take the stock back to the chopping block, and start shaping the outside using the traced lines and your eye. Use the small carving ax to shape the outside so that it reflects the bowl's inner surface (**R–S**). Remember to leave the ends of the bowl thicker, around ¾", for strength. Because the bottom and sides are parallel with the grain, they can remain thinner and still be strong. If you'd like, sand and plane the bowl a bit (**T–V**). Finish it with olive oil or edible flaxseed oil after is has dried slowly, away from heat.

# *All the Strength in the Wood:*
# HOOK

## JON STROM

Probably ever since humans first began to wear garments, we have felt a need to keep them off the floor, tidy and dry. The natural shapes in the branching birch tree have inspired various hook designs that help meet this need. Leaving the branch as it was grown or enhancing the shape with a little artful carving produces a smart and interesting solution to the problem of hanging up our belongings. Some of the more interesting designs can be found with multiple hooks on the same branch. This project can be done by first-time carvers or embellished in the hands of more experienced woodworkers.

## Materials

- ◆ Forked birch branch
- ◆ Small crosscut saw or coping saw
- ◆ Hatchet
- ◆ Plane (optional)
- ◆ Ax
- ◆ Sloyd or long-bladed carving knife
- ◆ Handheld power drill
- ◆ Drill bit suitable to size of hook
- ◆ Linseed oil or paint
- ◆ Screwdriver
- ◆ Mounting screws suitable to size of hook

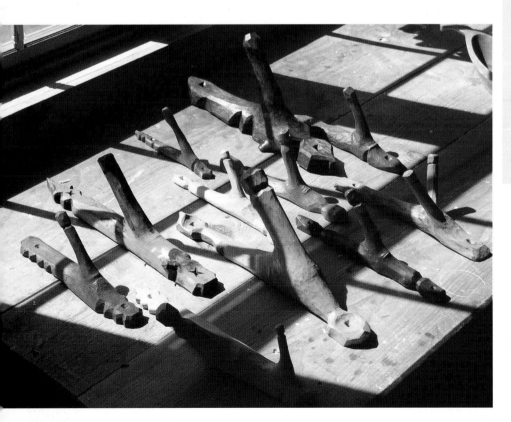

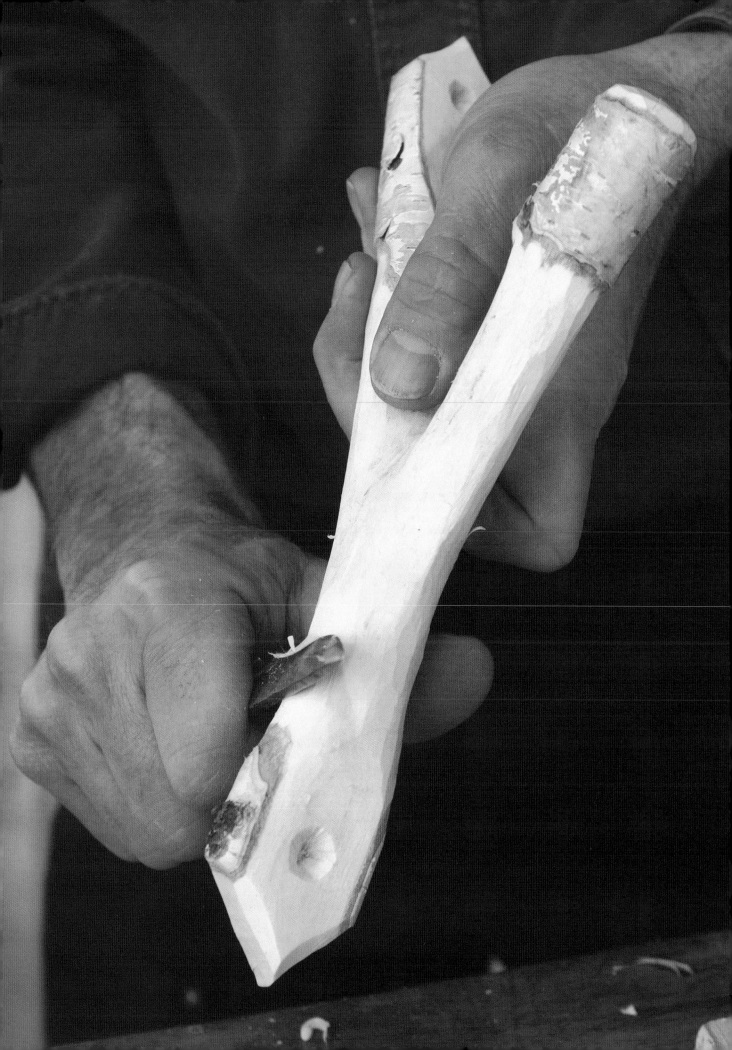

1. Select a forked birch branch with one straight side (**A**).

2. Saw the fork that will become the hook to a shorter length than the straight back, which will be screwed to a wall, door, or beam (**B**).

3. Flatten the back side of the hook with a sharp hatchet. Take off one-third to one-half of the thickness of the branch (**C–D**). True it by laying it on a flat surface to test your progression. Use a plane to flatten it, if necessary.

4. Use an ax to flatten the top and the bottom relatively parallel with the back where the holes will be drilled for mounting screws (**E–F**).

5. Use a knife to peel off as much bark as desired, just as you would peel a carrot (G–H).

6. Round off the end of the hook where the garment or towel will hang (I).

7. Use the knife to shape the sides, if desired, always making sure to carve with the grain of the wood. Leave the widest part where the holes for mounting will be drilled (J).

8. Using a power drill and a bit suitable to the size of your hook, drill holes for the mounting screws in the back of the hook. Then, smooth all cut surfaces with the sharp knife (K–M). When the wood has dried, finish the hook with linseed oil or paint, let it dry, and use a screwdriver to mount it in your favorite place.

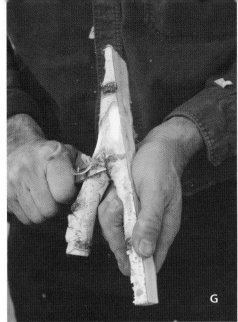

G

H

I

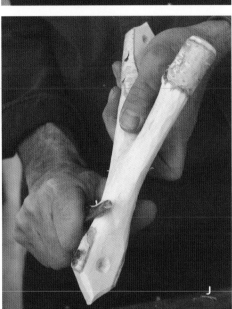

J

K

L

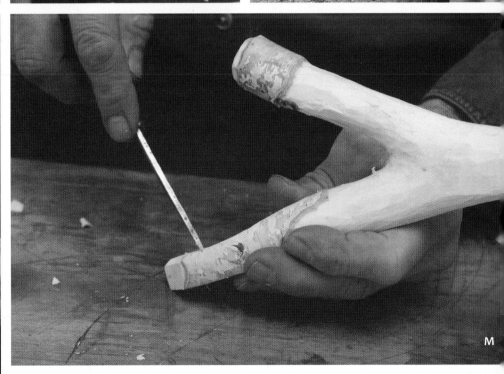

M

# Intrigue in Motion:
# SHRINK BOX

## JON STROM

Shrink boxes are made by scooping out the insides of a green wood sapling. As the resulting cylinder dries, it shrinks and locks the bottom piece in place. The process of making shrink boxes was originally shared with North House Folk School by Swedish instructors Anja Sundberg and Jögge Sundqvist, who like to paint their boxes in playful, friendly colors.

Using the natural shrinking of a log as it dries to close cracks and voids is quite a change from Jon Strom's normal experience with wood. After learning about the tradition of using this force to make a tight, lightweight box of birch, he was delighted to discover a use for the straight sections of branches that are usually discarded in the woods. The variations possible in the design and use for such containers are many. This challenge sets his intrigue in motion, causing him to find out what the next possibilities are as he makes more and more boxes.

## Materials

◆ Fresh green birch branch or small trunk

◆ Bow saw

◆ Carving knife

◆ Vise

◆ Hand or power drill

◆ 2" auger bit

◆ Pencil

◆ 2" gouge

◆ ¼" basswood board

◆ Coping saw

◆ ½" basswood board for lid (optional)

◆ 1 tbsp. flour (optional)

A

B

C

1. Using a saw, cut a fresh green birch branch or small trunk no bigger than the palm of your hand to be the body of the box (A–B).

2. With a knife, shape the outside to any desired shape or leave it in its natural round state with or without the bark. I decided to create a simple heptagon for my box (C–D).

3. Using a vise and a hand or power drill with a 2" auger bit, drill out the bulk of center wood from the branch or trunk (E).

4. With a pencil, scribe a line on the inside, leaving a wall thickness of about ¼". Carve away the inside to this even thickness using a 2" gouge and the knife (F–H).

5. Scribe a line inside the box (approximately ⅜" above the base) and another about ¼" from the base (I).

6. Using the tip of the knife, cut the line closest to the top of the box straight inward and parallel to its base. Cut the lower traced line at a 45-degree angle to meet the first cut. A V-shaped groove should remain (J–L).

D

E

F

G

H

I

7. Trace the inside bottom shape onto a ¼" dry basswood board (M). Cut this piece with a coping saw (N).

8. With the knife, chamfer the edge of this bottom piece to a 45-degree angle, cutting down from the top edge and leaving the top flat and full in diameter (O).

9. Trim this bottom as needed until it will fit as snugly as possible into the groove you previously cut. It will sit slightly loose until the "wet" green outer box shrinks around this dry bottom piece (P–Q).

10. Allow the box to dry slowly, away from direct heat. When the box has dried and shrunk, make a lid, if desired, out of dry basswood. To determine the size and shape of the lid, put a tablespoon of flour inside the box, place a wetted piece of ½" basswood over the opening, and turn the box and basswood together upside down (the basswood is now on the bottom). Turn the box and basswood together right side up and remove the basswood. The flour will be stuck to the wetted basswood, giving the size and shape of the lid. Cut out the lid with the coping saw. Carve a shoulder along the edge of the lid so that some wood hangs down inside the box, creating a snug fit. Admire your finished box (R)!

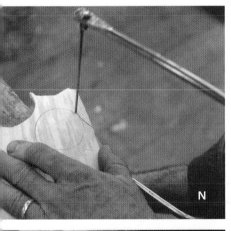

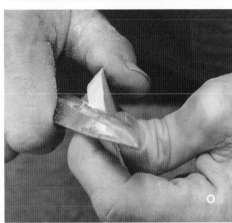

# *Magical Little Boxes:*
# BIRCH BOX

## FRED LIVESAY

Eighteenth- and nineteenth-century Scandinavians commonly kept small, flat birch bark boxes in their pockets for the then-popular taking of snuff. But snuff was not the only item kept in birch bark boxes; larger lapped-birch bark boxes often held coffee, tea, tobacco, salt, or even butter. The oldest known carbon 14–dated birch bark box was found in the summer of 1927 at a site in Ørlandet, Norway. It is in remarkable condition for being 2500 years-old. Further analysis determined it was probably used for butter. What might the archeaologists find in your boxes: . . . buttons, spare change, jewelery, a child's found treasures?

## Materials

- Fairly unblemished piece of birch bark, 3" wide x 21" long
- Scissors
- Carving knife
- Ruler
- Square (optional)
- Pencil
- Awl
- Two to four clothespins
- Four-in-one hand file
- Dry, straight-grained section of sapling, 2¼" diameter by 4" long, split in half lengthwise
- Two to four wedges, 4" long and same width as diameter of sapling
- Close-grained pine board, ¾" thick x 12" long x 3" wide for base and lid
- Japanese pull saw, coping saw, or hand saw with fine teeth
- Scorp (optional)
- Dry section of ash, birch, or thornapple branch, 1" diameter x 2" long for 4 trine nails
- Small hammer with 8- to 12-ounce head
- Needlenose pliers with wire cutter
- Paste wax or linseed oil (optional)

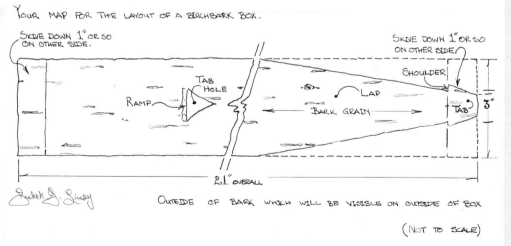

YOUR MAP FOR THE LAYOUT OF A BIRCHBARK BOX.

SKIVE DOWN 1" OR SO ON OTHER SIDE.

SKIVE DOWN 1" OR SO ON OTHER SIDE.

SHOULDER

TAB HOLE

RAMP

LAP

BARK GRAIN

TAB

3"

2.1" OVERALL

OUTSIDE OF BARK WHICH WILL BE VISIBLE ON OUTSIDE OF BOX

(NOT TO SCALE)

1. Choose a flat piece of bark that is fairly smooth and free of bumps ("wood hags," puckers, and waves.) Use scissors or a knife and straightedge to cut a strip from the bark about 3" wide, making the long edges as parallel as possible. Next, trim the ends of the strip as square to the top and bottom edges as you can. Use a square if needed.

2. Peel the papery white or gray outer bark from the bark strip, being careful to leave the bark piece as thick as possible, by holding the strip vertically between your legs, starting at the ends, and using your thumbs to separate the bark while your fingers hold both sides. Use the sharp knife to start if needed. Bark that will not peel to an even layer may be rubbed perpendicularly to the grain with your fingers or thumb to complete the peel (A–B). Use the carving knife, four-in-one hand rasp, or whatever tool fits the job to smooth out any bumps in the bark that might keep it from laying flat.

3. Face the side you just prepared toward you and begin rolling up the strip. When you roll up the bark so that it has three layers, it will have one end on the inside of the roll and another on the outside of the roll. Each end will face the opposite way of the other and should overlap. The total overlap will be 2" or so (an inch in each direction) with a layer of bark between the two ends. This will be the approximate size of your finished box (C).

4. Hold the box in one hand, as you would a glass of water, being careful not to let the bark unroll. Use clothespins to keep it from unrolling if necessary. With a sharp pencil or an awl, mark where the end of the strip lies on the inside of the box. Next, make a small mark at the approximate center of the other end of the strip on the outside of the box. The exact center will be determined in the next step. Also mark which side is on the outside and which side is on the inside of the box.

5. Unroll the bark strip, peeled side away from you and lay it flat. Weight the end if it wants to curl up. Locate the end that was on the outside of the box and the mark you made. With your ruler and pencil or awl, find the exact center of the strip and make another mark on the bark (not too big or it may show up later) about ⅜" in from the first mark.

6. Turn the bark over so the peeled side faces you. Using the ruler, locate the end of the bark previously on the inside of the box and draw a line across it about 1" to 1¼" in from the end.

7. With the peeled side still facing you, go to the other end of the bark strip and use the ruler to divide the strip lengthwise in thirds. Mark these thirds with two small dashes, running lengthwise. Repeat this process about one inch in from the end and connect the dashes using the ruler and the awl or pencil. You should have three 1" wide by about 1" long strips marked on this end of the bark. The center third is the tab. Next, draw a perpendicular line one inch in from the end to establish the shoulder of the tab and the end of the lap. Measure about ⅛" above and below the central third, and mark it with an awl or a pencil (D).

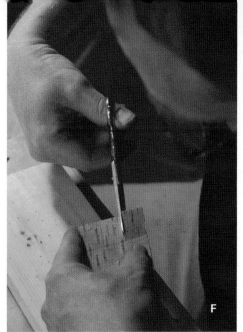
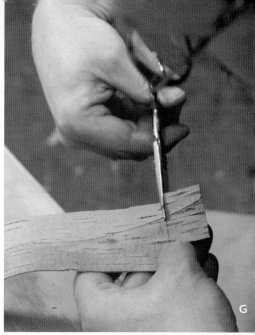

8. Keeping the bark flat, measure back from the same end of the strip you've just marked, a little more than half of the length of the entire strip of bark. Make two small marks at the upper and lower edge of the long strip on the peeled side.

9. Place the edge of the ruler along one side of the tab and the rough halfway mark you just made in Step 8 (E); connect the points with the pencil or awl. Repeat this step for the lower side of the strip. You should now have drawn your tapered lap that ends at the tab shoulder line. You are now ready to cut the shoulders, the lap, and the tab.

10. To create this arrow with a blunt end, use scissors to cut from the outside edge along the shoulder line. If you are using the knife, start from the inside and cut to the outside edge. Stop the cut about ¹⁄₁₆" from the intersection of the lap and the tab shoulder. Start cutting the tapered lap. Be careful not to cut too far or the tab shoulder may split and you will have to start the layout over again (F–G). Lastly, taper the tab slightly with the knife. Your tab and lap should look like the one in photo H.

11. To make the triangular tab hole into which the arrow locks, start by rolling up the box, returning to the initial layout marks of Steps 3 and 4. Use clothespins to keep the bark from unrolling. Take the awl in one hand and hold the tab against the box with the other. Sneak the awl point just under the barb of the arrow and mark it by pressing the awl lightly into the bark. This is where the tapered lap and the tab shoulders meet. Now, sneak the point of the awl about ⅛" in under the center of the tip of the blunt end of the arrow and make a mark. Remove the clothespins and unroll the bark (I–J).

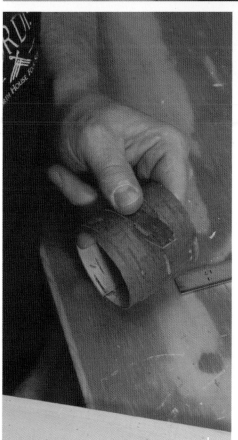
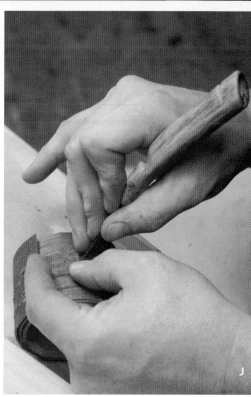

K

L

12. Lay the bark flat with the unpeeled side facing up and weight the bark if needed to keep it from curling up. Holding the carving knife like pencil, connect the three marks left by the poi of the awl. The triangular hole should look like the one in photo **K**.

13. Use your knife tip to create a ramp for the last ¼" to ⅜" of the lap so it has a smooth transition into the tab hole. The ramp should bevel gentl at the base of the triangle (**L–N**). Test fit the tab and the tab hole. You can always make the hol a bit bigger. Patience and trial and error are key.

14. Once the tab is fit to the tab hole, undo the bo Skive, or thin down to a taper, the first 1" of eac end of the bark with your knife. You may also use the four-in-one file to make the tapers. Be careful not to make the barbs on the tab too thin or it will not hold when you stretch your box tight. Do all skiving on the peeled side of the bark (**O–P**).

M

N

O

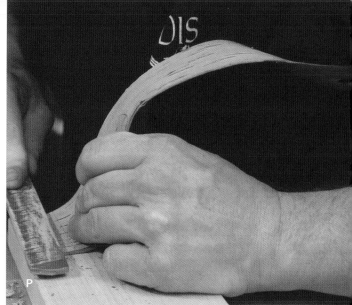

P

15. Put the box together for the final fit as in Step 13. Take the tail end of the bark strip and roll it up tightly as seen in **Q**. Let go of the bark and help it to unroll and lie smoothly against the other layers (**R**). Gently pull the tab against the tab hole to lock the bark in place. Don't pull too hard, or you may pull the tab from the tab hole and snap the shoulders of the tab.

16. Once the box is fitted together, expand the bark by inserting the sapling halves, which may be carved down to fit inside the box. Next, insert the wedges from each side as needed to tighten and stretch the box. Leave box with stretchers for two days, checking now and then to tighten the wedges. Use only hand pressure during these steps (**S–U**).

V

W

17. Remove the wedges and stretchers after two days and begin working on a base and lid. Make sure the skived-down end of bark on the inside of the box is opposite the outside tab. Orient the box on a pine board with the grain running the length of the oval box. Trace the inside of the box base on the wood with the pencil (V). Label the bottom of the box on both the bark and the base. Cut out the base roughly with a saw, leaving the pencil line (W). Carve the base to fit using trial and error. Your base may be shouldered (X–Z) or flush fit and hollowed with a scorp (AA). The bottom fits correctly when the base squeaks home when inserted into the bark and no light is visible when looking inside the box. Repeat this process with the lid. The lid may have also have a shoulder or lip or leather tab for a handle and should "pop" when fitted correctly (V–AA).

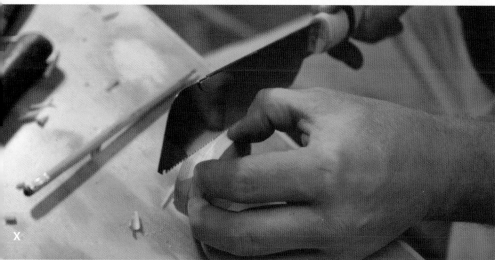

X

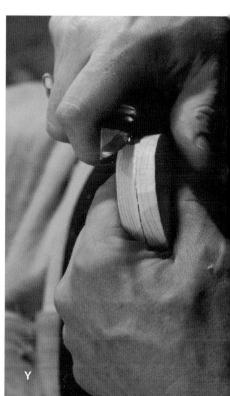

Y

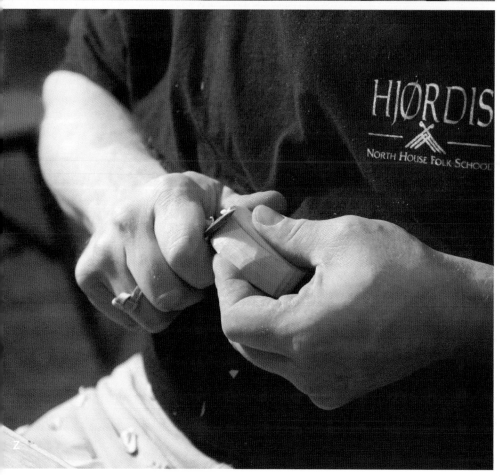

HJØRDIS

NORTH HOUSE FOLK SCHOOL

Z

AA

18. To secure the base and bark, begin by using the awl to make six to eight evenly spaced holes about ⅜" deep through the bark and into the base for the wooden pegs. A square or diamond blade awl works best (BB). Next, find a tough, dry, straight, and tight-grained piece of wood and cut a piece about an inch long. Use your knife and a block of wood as a mallet to split off the square pegs (CC). Pegs can be used square or carved (DD–EE), but all must be pointed on their ends like nails. I sometimes put heads on my pegs. Pegs should be only slightly bigger than the holes made with the awl. If pegs are too big, they may split the base, and you will have to make a new one. Use a small hammer to set the pegs. Make sure the base is backed up by the work surface opposite the peg you are driving (FF). Trim off any pegs that stand proud of the bark with a wire cutter, leaving 1/16" of the peg above the bark. Gently peen the peg with the hammer to create a burr or head.

19. The completed box may be given a very light coat of paste wax or linseed oil or left unfinished (GG).

20. Put the lid on the box, admire, admire it a little more, and see what you might improve upon or change. Then, start your next box.

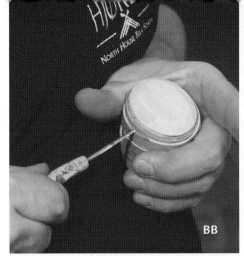

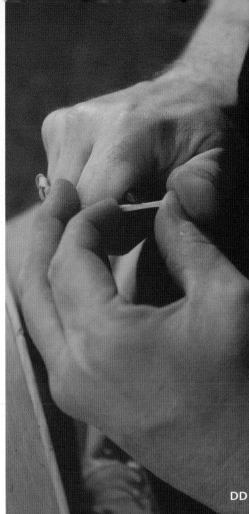

**BB**

**DD**

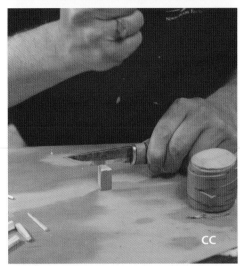

**CC**

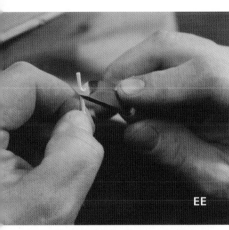

**EE**

**FF**

**GG**

# The Craftsmanship of Risk:
# TURNED BOWL

## ROGER ABRAHAMSON

Ale bowls were common utensils on farms and in homes of the past in northern Europe and America. Most families had one big communal bowl that sat in the center of their table. The oldest wooden bowl currently known was found in Italy and dates back to 700 BC.

Turning a bowl is simply a learned skill set, no different from learning to make a sandwich. It's the craftsmanship of risk, much like North House's entire vision. If you make a mistake and go all the way through the wood, there's no need to worry . . . you're simply left with a strainer. And you always have the opportunity to try again.

## Materials

- ◆ Green birch log, length equal to diameter
- ◆ Small broad ax or side hatchet
- ◆ Carving ax
- ◆ Dividers
- ◆ Brace and ¾" spoon or other drill bit
- ◆ Mandrel with ¾" round tenon
- ◆ Small piece of birch bark
- ◆ Spring pole lathe
- ◆ Larger straight-shaft hook tool
- ◆ Small curved-shaft hook tool
- ◆ Carving scorp or hook knife
- ◆ Paper bag
- ◆ Sandpaper
- ◆ Linseed oil (optional)

1. Begin with a green birch log cut approximately to the same length as its diameter. Remove the bark and split the log in half with a broad ax (**A**).

2. Using the broad ax, true up the log's face (**B**). Switch to a carving ax and chop the log into a hemisphere shape, making certain to cut with the grain. Remove all bark and arrive as close to round as possible (**C–D**).

3. Locate the center of the bowl using dividers (**E**)

4. To ready the bowl for the lathe, bore a hole at this center point with a brace and spoon bit and drive the tenon of the mandrel into the hole. Wedge with a small piece of birch bark if necessary (**F–G**).

5. Place the bowl and mandrel between the centers of the lathe, wrapping the drive cord around the mandrel and centering the assembly to rotate as close as possible to true. Orient the bowl so the exterior is on the right-hand side of the lathe (on most lathes). Secure the lathe centers (**H**).

6. Begin turning. Rough out the exterior using the larger straight hook tool. Work from the base to the rim in order to shape with the grain. To get a clean cut, be sure the hook tool goes into, through, and then exits the wood with each stroke of the treadle, much the way you would peel an apple (I–K).

7. Once the bowl begins to take shape, again use the carving ax to remove excess wood (L–M).

8. Complete roughing out the exterior, turn the bowl-mandrel assembly end-for-end in the lathe, and using a small curved hook tool, true up the face of the bowl (N).

9. At the point closest to the mandrel, cut a groove using a plunge cut with the small hook tool (O).

H

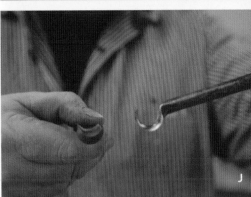

I

J

K

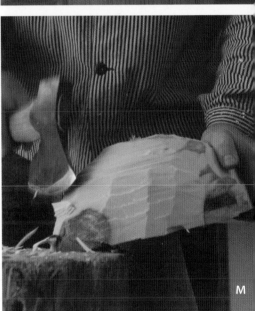

L

M

N

O

P

Q

10. Switch back to the bowl's exterior and decide where to place the foot (it usually rests in the center). At this point, using a carving scorp and the small hook tool, cut straight in, parallel to the centerline, to the desired depth. Blend in the foot cut with the exterior shape (P). Hollow the inside of the foot slightly (Q). Flatten the foot rim.

11. Stop to sharpen your tools often (R).

12. After sharpening your tools, fine-tune the outside of the bowl, working from foot to "lip" (S–T). Leave a rim and collar if desired, and burnish the outside of the bowl with shavings (U).

13. Flip the bowl again and continue hollowing the inside of the bowl, alternating between the large and small hook tools. An ideal thickness is ¼". Arrive at the smoothest bowl possible (V).

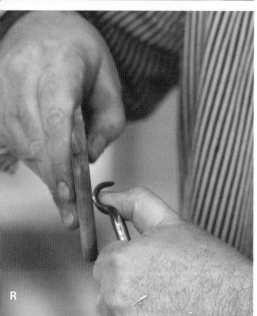

R

S

T

U

4. Now, begin working to remove the core, undercutting very close to the bottom of the bowl (**W**).

5. Once ready, break off the core, or "bellybutton", from the bowl (**X**).

6. Using the carving scorp, work across the grain to get rid of the leftover core (**Y–Z**). Relax after doing this, and congratulate yourself after standing and working so diligently. To dry the bowl, place it in a paper bag for two weeks. When it is fully dry, make any final smoothing with the knife and then sand it with sandpaper, starting with a coarse grit and moving up toward a finer grit. If you wish, finish with linseed oil.

V

W

X

Y

Z

# *Throwing Logs:*
# KUBB

## KURT MEAD

When Kurt Mead and his wife were in Sweden a few years ago, they observed growing excitement over a "new" game that was taking the country by storm. The game was called Kubb, which means "log" in Swedish, and it was being played at picnics, reunions, birthday parties . . . just about every type of backyard event in Sweden. However, the game of "throwing logs" isn't exactly new. While some say it originated in twentieth-century Scandinavia, others claim that it was played as far back as 770 AD by the Vikings (hence its other name—Viking chess).

Scandinavia is not richly populated with a variety of native hardwoods. However, the birch tree is abundant there, and it holds a prominent place in Scandinavian culture. So while Kubb sets can be fabricated from just about any hardwood, it seems only fitting to make this project from birch.

## Materials

- ◆ Birch lumber to accommodate all 21 pieces

  **Note:** Birch lumber, in various sizes, can be special-ordered from most home centers if it is not already in stock. Specialty lumberyards and local sawmills may be able to custom mill the appropriate sizes. Other woods may be substituted if birch is not available. Birch lumber that contains any knots will warp as it dries. The dimensions below and step-by-step instructions that follow are written with the assumption that the lumber used is straight and true.

  There are 21 pieces in a Kubb set:
  - 10 Kubbs: 2½" x 2½" x 6"
  - 6 Batons: 1½" x 1½" x 12" octagonal
  - 4 Corner posts: 1" x 1" x 12"
  - 1 King: 3¼" x 3¼" x 12"

- ◆ Router (optional)
- ◆ Table saw
- ◆ Belt sander, grinder, or medium-grit sandpaper
- ◆ Hatchet (optional)

8m (26 ft)   5m (16 ft)

*Kurt Mead*

This game contains 21 game pieces made of solid wood, with each set made up of the following:

- ◆ 10 Kubbs
- ◆ 6 Batons
- ◆ 4 Corner posts
- ◆ 1 King

Kubb requires 21 game pieces made of solid wood. This set, made by Kurt Mead, is constructed of birch, the most abundant species of hardwood in Scandinavia, the birthplace of Kubb.

## FIELD

The game is played on a field that measures 5 m x 8 m (approximately 16' x 26'). The four corner posts are used to mark the corners. Field size can be adjusted smaller to fit the topography and the players' skill or age.

## SETUP

Five Kubbs are set up, evenly spaced, along the baselines (short sides) of each end of the field. The King is placed in the center.

## TEAMS

The two teams are made up of between one and six players each.

## GOAL

Knock down all of your opponents' Kubbs, followed by the King.

## STARTING THE GAME

Each team throws one baton toward the King. The team whose baton lands closest to the King without toppling him gets to start.

## OFFENSIVE PLAY

The first team starts by throwing the six batons at their opponents' baseline Kubbs. You must throw from behind the baseline, and you may not throw from outside the corner posts. Batons are held at one end and are thrown underhand. Tempting though it may be, players are not allowed to grip the baton in the middle, to throw it overhand, or to "helicopter" the baton.

The King can only be toppled if you have downed your opponents' entire baseline of Kubbs. You only get one chance (one baton) to drop the King. If you fail, all six batons are given to the opposing team, and it is then their play. If you knock over the King at any other time during the game, you instantly lose the game.

When all six batons have been thrown, play switches to the other team.

## DEFENSIVE PLAY

The second team must retrieve any Kubbs knocked over by their opponents and make them into field Kubbs before taking their turn at throwing the batons. To make the fallen Kubbs into field Kubbs, the second team picks up the toppled Kubbs and tosses them into their opponents' half of the field. Each Kubb must come to rest within the boundaries of that half of the field. You get only two chances to throw each Kubb into the field. If on the second try your Kubb lands outside the boundaries, your opponents may place the Kubb wherever they want, but at least one baton-length away from the King.

From the location where each Kubb lies, your opponents will choose which end tips up and they will upright all field Kubbs as they are thrown. If the thrown Kubb contacts an upended field Kubb, the two Kubbs are stacked into a T-shaped tower at the location of the upright field Kubb. It is possible to have more than two Kubbs in a tower.

Before going on the offensive and trying to knock over your opponents' Kubbs, you must retrieve your own field Kubbs by knocking them over with your six batons. Any baseline (opponents' original) Kubbs accidentally tipped before all field Kubbs are toppled will be immediately uprighted. As soon as all field Kubbs are knocked over, offensive play may resume. Any field Kubbs not knocked over are left on the field for the next round, leaving fewer baseline Kubbs for your opponents to knock down. Those knocked down are tossed back to the other side.

When all batons are thrown, play switches back to the first team.

## CONTINUED PLAY

The first team picks up the toppled field Kubbs and tosses them to their opponents' side of the field where their opponents set them up. If the second team left any field Kubbs standing, the first team may use the location of the second team's centermost (closest to your opponents' baseline) field Kubb as the new casting line from which to retrieve field Kubbs and attack baseline Kubbs. Note that all 10 Kubbs are always on the field. Playing pieces are not removed during play.

Play continues until one team knocks down all five of their opponents' Kubbs, followed by the King.

1. About 6' of 2½" x 2½" birch stock is needed for the Kubbs, which are the "soldiers" of the game. You'll need five of these short, stout blocks for each team, or ten total. With a router or table saw, gently chamfer or round the edges (A). Cut ten 6"-long pieces. Chamfer or round the square edges on the tops and bottoms (B). Taking off the sharp edges will reduce the chance of chipping or splitting the edges of the pieces during play.

2. Adjust the table saw blade to 45 degrees. You will need 6' plus of 1½" x 1½" birch stock to make the batons, which are used in offensive play. They will be octagonal in cross section. Move the ripping fence to a position that will allow the 90-degree edges of the stock to be ripped in such a way that all eight sides are approximately the same width (C–D).

A

B

C

D

131

3. Cut the octagonal rod into six 12" lengths. Mark line 12" from the saw blade as a guide for cutting the batons. Gently round the square edges on the ends of the batons with a belt sander, a grinder, or by hand with sandpaper (E–F).

4. The four corner posts are used to mark the corners of the playing field and can be ripped from scrap pieces left over from making the other pieces. Dimensions of 1" x 1" x 12" seem to work well, but use what you have. Chamfer the edges of the stock to match the Kubbs, and cut them into about 12" lengths (G). Sharpen one end of the post with the table saw or a sharp hatchet.

5. A 12" length of 3¼" x 3¼" birch is all that is needed for the King (H). The top of the King is traditionally cut into a crown shape. The simplest crown has four points, but a skilled woodworker can figure out how to cut a handsome, nine-pointed crown. To cut a four-pointed crown, two opposing 45-degree angle cuts will be made in the top of the King to form a V-shaped groove (I). Start by adjusting the ripping fence about ¼" from the blade. Raise the table saw blade, at a 45-degree angle, to a depth at which the opposing cuts will meet perfectly at the apex of the V. Use scrap material to test the depth of the cuts, adjusting the blade height until the proper depth is achieved. Chamfer or round the edges of the King in the same way and to the same extent as the Kubbs. To delineate the King's crown, cut a shallow V-shaped groove on each side with intersecting 45-degree-angle cuts (J).

6. Sand and touch up the pieces, but don't be afraid to leave them a bit rustic. They're going to get beat up as you use them (K).

# Finding the Heart:
# DALA HORSE

## HARLEY REFSAL

Scandinavian carvers have created small, handheld wooden horses for centuries. But it was the men of the Swedish province of Dalarna who first began to carve Dala horses in the early decades of the 1800s, when they spent long weeks away in the woods during the winter, felling trees for sawmills. During the evenings, tightly crammed into makeshift bunkhouses, they whittled horses. The pastime became a well-established tradition. Today, in the village of Nusnäs, more than 250,000 Dala horses are individually carved and painted each year, making the popular critter Sweden's unofficial national symbol.

North House Folk School instructor Harley Refsal began to carve in the late 1960s and has been going ever since. Although he's now internationally recognized and celebrated, Harley learned his craft as anyone can—by watching, observing, and experiencing.

*Materials*

- Freshly felled birch
- Ax or splitting wedge
- Pencil
- Horse pattern
- Band saw or handsaw
- Carving knife
- 3 brown paper bags
- Paint (optional)

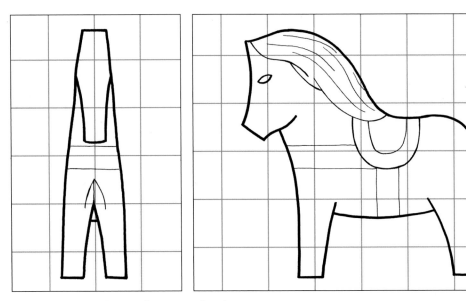

Each square equals one inch. Pattern shown at 50% of actual size.

© Harley Refsal

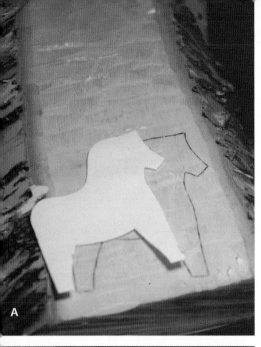

A

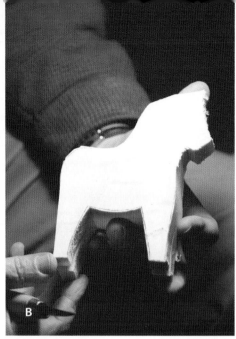

B

1. Using an ax or splitting wedge, split a piece of freshly felled birch to at least 5½" x 5½" x 1¾" thick. Trace the horse pattern onto the wood, with the grain direction running along the thinnest (and therefore potentially weakest) area: the legs (A).

2. Saw out the profile using a band saw or a handsaw (B).

3. Use a carving knife to begin to carve off sharp corners, rounding the horse's body. Work from the corners in (C–D).

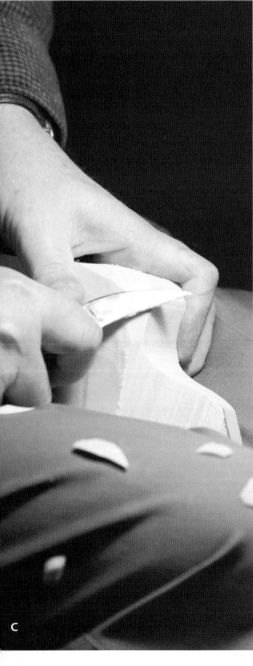

C

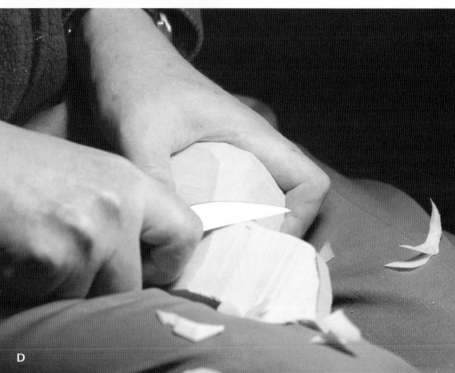

D

E

F

4. Taper the legs to achieve a trimmer, lighter look. This is an important cut, making the horse come alive from its otherwise relatively vague animal state (E–F).

5. Thin the neck area (G–H).

6. Continue by rounding the underbelly and the back of the horse. Remember that to capture the Scandinavian style of carving, you want to leave flat planes, or facets, in the wood (I–K).

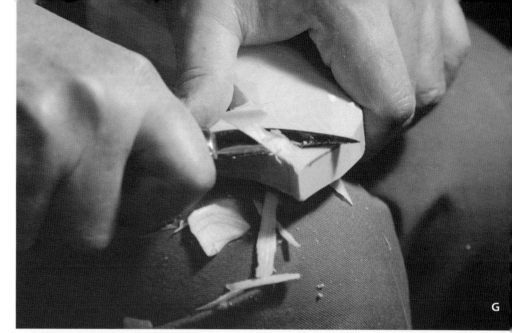

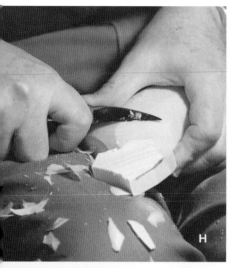

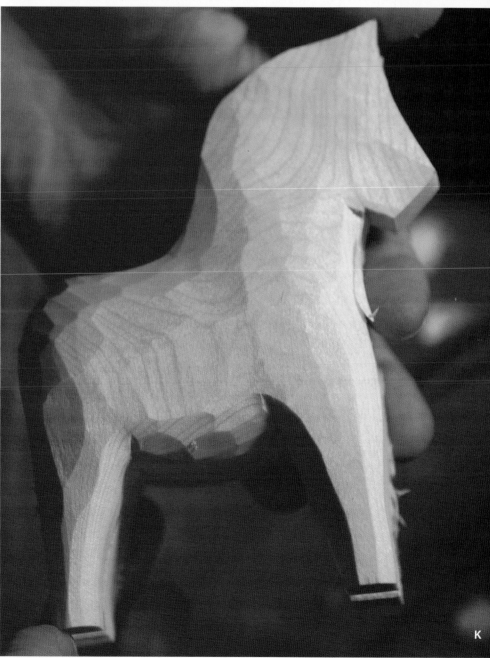

7. Continue to taper and shape the legs by creating more planes on the fronts, backs, and sides of the legs. Deepen the separation between the two front legs as well as the two hind legs (L).

8. Continue to finish carve around the entire horse (M–P). **Note:** The finished horse must now be dried under controlled conditions. If simply left out in the open air, the fresh, moist wood will crack as it dries. Place the horse into paper bag #1, roll the bag shut, place that bag into paper bag #2, roll that bag shut, and then place that bag into paper bag #3. The three layers of paper will wick the moisture out of the fresh wood, but at a slow, controlled rate so that cracking should not occur. After a few days (or a few weeks, depending on humidity and temperature), unpack the horse to check on the drying process. To determine if the carving is dry, tap it with a hard, nonmarring object, such as a heavy metal ladle or spoon. After the carving is thoroughly dried and cured, the wood will produce a sharp "click" sound rather than the dull "thud" sound produced when striking wet, freshly cut wood.

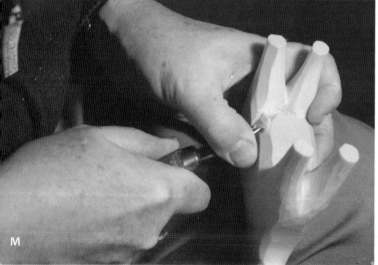

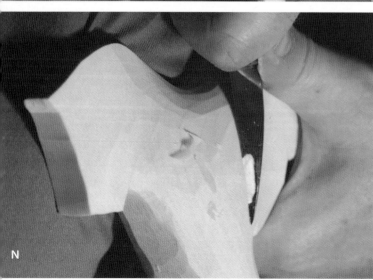

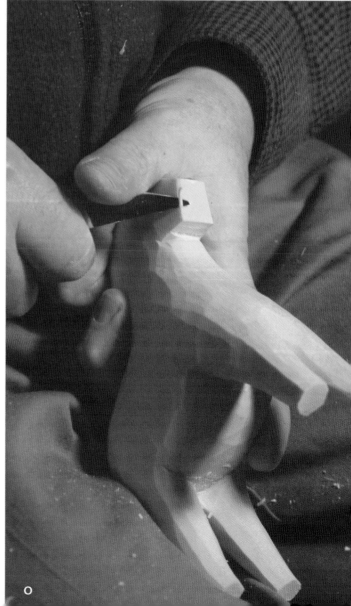

9. Fine details, such as eyes and decorative elements, can now be carved in. Be sure to sign your finished carving (**Q**). Paint if you wish, making certain to let the paint dry properly before displaying the finished carving.

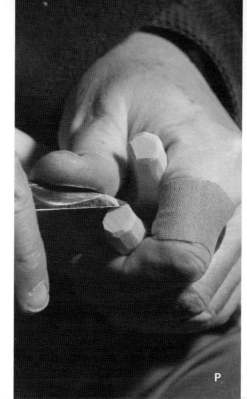

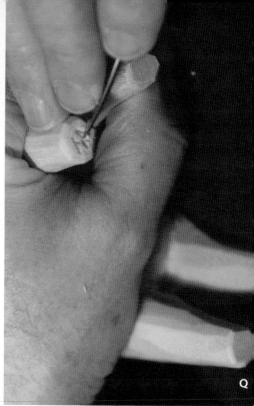

# FINDING THE HEART

*Betsy Bowen, artist*

Growing up, I often heard the story of Peter and Trott-trott, the little wooden Swedish horse that was just like my very own painted horse that my father had given me. Peter fed his horse every day, and it grew! One day Trott-trott was big enough to ride and took Peter on an adventure very far from home. As they rode through the hills and forests, they came upon people whose colorful clothes looked like the bright paintings on the horse, until finally they arrived at the workshop of the old woodcarver who had made Trott-trott. Here is what the woodcarver said when he had heard the whole story: "Every tree has a heart, and if you find the heart, it comes alive in the wood, whether in a horse or a chair or a fiddle."

Woodcut. Betsy Bowen, Minnesota, 2001.

139

# BIRCH'S BIOLOGY AND ECOLOGY

**"WHAT IS THIS TREE SPECIES THAT HAS BEEN SUCH AN IMPORTANT PART OF NORTH HOUSE FOLK SCHOOL'S FIRST DECADE?"**
—*John Zasada, forester and instructor*

Throughout the ages, birch has played an important role in culture and history. Today, birch trees often define the character of the woods in northern climates and are a part of traditional handcrafts wherever they grow. Though we can't look into a crystal ball to see what lies ahead, there are some current developments and important issues to consider that directly and indirectly relate to what the future holds for the birch.

# UNDERSTANDING BIRCH, ITS USES, AND ITS FUTURE

## JOHN ZASADA

More than just knowing the birch's place in our lore, history, and crafts, a complete understanding of this tree has to include its biology, ecology, and place in our lives, both now and in the future. For the collectors and makers of birch handcrafts, this knowledge is specifically important for the responsible harvesting of the tree and its many parts.

When we talk about birch, we mean trees from the genus *Betula*, which includes all the species of birch that occur in North America and the rest of the Northern Hemisphere. A recent study of birch distribution indicates that there are about 16 birch species in North America and 35 species worldwide. The birch family is generally divided into three groups by botanists, taxonomists, and ecologists. The first group contains the largest trees and is represented in northern Minnesota by the yellow birch. The second group includes the dwarf, or shrub, birch and incorporates the bog birch. The third group is composed of trees often referred to as "white-barked" birches, including the paper birch, *Betula papyrifera*—a tree that is of particular interest for us in the North Woods due to its use in our traditional crafts.

## THE WHITE-BARKED BIRCHES

At one time, all of the white-barked birch in North America was considered *Betula papyrifera*. Making identification even more difficult is the birch's ability to readily hybridize with other birch species; however, more recent classification work divides this transcontinental "complex" into four or five species.

Even though their current classification now divides them, all white-barked birch species still share two major characteristics—the harvesting of their white outer bark and the collection of their sap. Throughout the range of

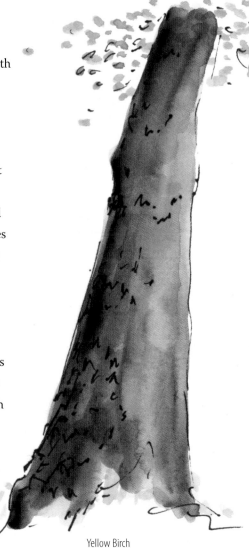

Yellow Birch

the white-barked birches, the outer bark has been gathered for centuries and used in many ways. Similarly, large quantities of birch sap have been harvested annually throughout Russia, Ukraine, Korea, Japan, and Finland. The near absence of birch sap collection in the southern part of their North American range is likely due to the presence of maple trees.

## WHERE SHE GROWS

Birch is a native of the temperate Northern Hemisphere. Although they have a significant range within the contiguous United States, birches are really a "northern" species, meaning they cover and are most common in the sub-boreal and boreal forests around the Northern Hemisphere.

Birch growth occurs in a wide range of soil conditions within its transcontinental North American range, from the permafrost in Alaska to the rich soils of the northern hardwood forests in the Great Lakes region and northeastern United States. Birch grows best on warmer, south-facing sites in the far north and mixed with northern hardwoods on richer sites

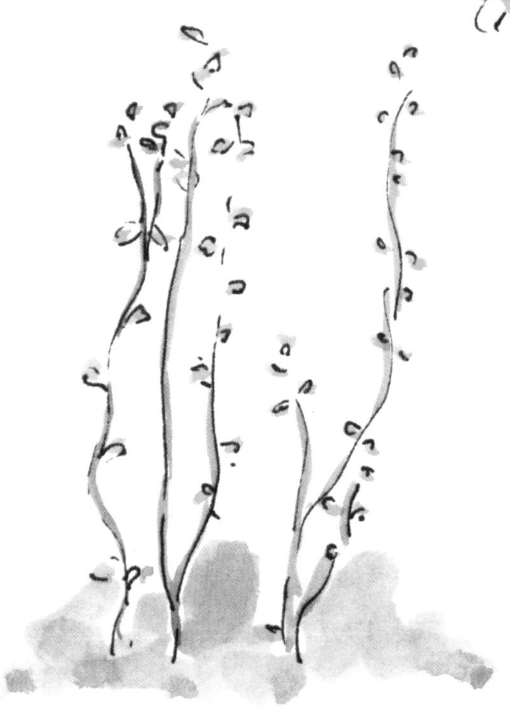

Bog Birch

White-Barked Birch

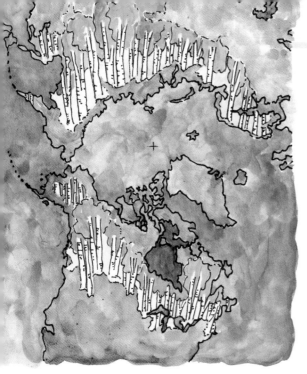

Distribution of white-barked birches in the Northern Hemisphere.

in the northern United States. Often, the competition yielded by other deciduous trees on a productive site will increase the difficulty of growing paper birch; other hardwoods are usually more shade tolerant and can regenerate under lower light conditions than birch can. Thus, it can be difficult to establish birch regeneration if there is a significant amount of shading that other hardwoods and shrubs can tolerate but that birch cannot. In the Grand Marais area of Minnesota, for instance, pure stands of paper birch occur on sandy soils that are commonly occupied by red and white pines. The presence of these nearly pure stands of birch is related to past history of logging, fire, and other human disturbance more than to soil conditions.

## HER RELATIVES AND ASSOCIATES

Birch can grow in pure stands, but is most often found mixed in with other species. The other genera of the *Betulaceae* family—alder, hazel, hop hornbeam, and ironwood—are commonly found growing with the birch.

Alders (*Alnus*) are tall shrubs that can reach tree stature; they grow on both upland and lowland sites. Best known for their occurrence in lowland alder "swamps," their main claim to fame is their relationship with a species of fungus that allows them to take elemental nitrogen from the atmosphere and turn it into the type of nitrogen that plants use.

Hazels (*Corylus*) are medium-to-tall shrubs that occupy hardwood and conifer forests; they are notorious for creating dense, junglelike understories in pine and aspen stands. Periodically, they produce large crops of hazelnuts—a food source highly prized by various wildlife species.

The remaining two relatives—hop hornbeam (*Carpinus*) and ironwood (*Ostrya*)—are small- to medium-sized trees that usually grow mixed with other deciduous trees and are well-known by woodworkers for their very hard wood.

If you've ever traveled across the range of the white-barked birches from northern Minnesota to northern Canada or Alaska, you've probably noticed the broad array of forest types

Alder
*Alnus*

and species mixtures in which birch occurs. The diversity of tree species gradually declines with increasing latitude. In northern Minnesota, Wisconsin, and Michigan, it is not uncommon to find paper birch growing with 10 to 15 other tree species within 30 acres. These species might include sugar and red maples; white ash; basswood; yellow birch; ironwood; red oak; quaking and big tooth aspens; balsam poplar; balsam fir; red, white, and jack pines; and white spruce. By the time one arrives in Alaska, only aspen, white spruce, and less commonly black spruce, tamarack, or balsam poplar remain as common associates of birch. Regardless of latitude, the number of species of paper birch in the forest are dependent on the soil and history of natural and human disturbance on the site.

Hazel
*Corylus*

Hop Hornbeam
*Carpinus*

Ironwood
*Ostrya*

## GROWTH AND REGENERATION

Birch is a fairly resilient species—more so than her common associates. Resiliency refers to a tree's ability to recover following a natural or human disturbance. To eliminate birch from our forests would be almost impossible, given current forest management practices and environmental conditions.

Birch is usually classified as an early-succession tree species: this means that it occupies recently disturbed areas, has light and easily transported seeds, and requires almost full sunlight. Open conditions with almost full sunlight suit the birch best; therefore, following severe disturbances that expose and disturb the ground, such as fire or forest harvesting, birch can thrive. Additionally, the species grows rapidly during the first 25 to 30 years of life. During this period of swift growth, birch tends to be a dominant species, overshadowing slower-growing tree species. Eventually, those slow-but-steady growers catch up and may replace birch unless a disturbance occurs that starts the cycle over. Birch trees, relatively short-lived, generally live to be 60 to 80 years old, but occasionally survive more than 100 years. Common associates such as red and white pines, white spruce, and sugar maple, however, can live for several hundred years. Today's mature and overmature birch stands originated following disturbances that occurred 50 to 100 years ago: forest fires, clearing for agriculture and subsequent abandonment, and forest harvesting.

A traditional Ojibwe winter birch bark basket etched with a herringbone pattern and laced with spruce root. Loan courtesy of Grand Portage National Monument.

Generally speaking, the disturbance created during a logging operation in the summer will result in more good spots for birch to grow than those created during a winter harvest operation, as unfrozen summer ground is more likely to be disturbed during the process of cutting and removing the trees. Even the disturbance caused during summer logging will not likely be enough to generate pure birch forests. However, these summer disturbances will likely be sufficient to maintain the current distribution of birch in the northern forest.

This sunlit birch grove shows trees regenerated primarily from seed.

When open, sunny ground is available, birch regenerates in two ways: sexual and vegetative reproduction. Sexual reproduction is synonymous with seed germination, while vegetative regeneration occurs through basal sprouting. Sprouting occurs when a tree is cut or experiences a loss in vigor; buds at the base of the tree produce 10 to 20 shoots, which gradually thin to fewer stems as weaker sprouts die. In areas where birch was present before logging or fire, there is often a combination of trees originating from seeds and sprouting. Early growth of sprouts is always more rapid than seedling growth.

Mineral soil exposure is necessary for healthy birch growth. The most natural way to expose soil is through the use of prescribed fire, although this is not very common. More frequently, machines are used to create these conditions; they can create a variety of growing spaces, ranging from small areas of exposed soil to large continuous strips.

Baskets. Dennis Chilcote, Minnesota, 2006.

## A SHORT BOTANY LESSON

Before we talk about the birch's uses and how to harvest it, let's discuss the anatomy of the tree. From the heartwood to the sap, every part of the birch plays an important role. In particular, we want to look at a cross section of the main stem to understand the structure of the wood and bark.

### *Wood and Bark Structure*

The layer between the bark and the wood is the cambium. This thin sheath of cells is the growing part of the tree and produces the annual ring of wood (the xylem) on the inside and an annual but much thinner layer of inner bark (the phloem) on the outside. These annual layers of wood and bark serve several important functions. The xylem and phloem carry water and nutrients from the soil to the leaves. Additionally, the phloem distributes the products of photosynthesis from their origin in the leaves to the other living parts of the tree. The accumulation of inner bark layers also helps to protect the tree from insect and disease attacks.

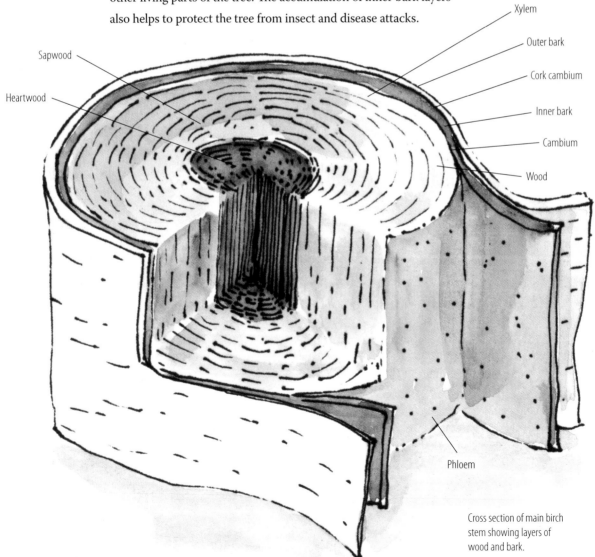

Xylem

Outer bark

Cork cambium

Inner bark

Cambium

Wood

Sapwood

Heartwood

Phloem

Cross section of main birch stem showing layers of wood and bark.

Although difficult in other trees, identifying and separating the inner layer of birch bark from the outer bark is relatively simple. The outer bark forms from the activity of the cork cambium, a thin layer of cells between the inner and outer bark. Each year, the cork cambium produces a thin layer of outer bark. As birch trees age, the older layers of outer bark begin to peel naturally, causing the shaggy appearance that is common in birch. Although tempting, peeling off the shaggy layers to start a campfire is a poor reason to damage the tree; keep in mind that you need permission to strip bark for any reason. The outer bark protects against insects and disease, bark stripping by herbivores, and physical damage from falling tree parts. It is filled with a battery of chemicals that defend against these attackers, and can also heal when it is damaged—not unlike a scab on our skin.

Dormant birch buds.

Birch wood is "diffuse porous," meaning that instead of having many large vessels concentrated in one part of the annual ring for transporting water—as in oak or ash—birch has many smaller vessels. There are also many thick-walled cells that assist with water transport and give the wood strength to support the "food factory" found in the leaves.

A cross section of a tree will often reveal a dark inner core of wood (heartwood) surrounded by a lighter-colored outer cylinder (sapwood). Flow of water occurs through the outer "dead" layers of the sapwood.

## Buds

The branching system in a tree is a direct result of the formation, growth, and fate of its buds. The buds either play their normal role, producing leaves and new branch growth, or are stopped before they can perform this function, either by being eaten by a bird or squirrel or breaking off in a windstorm.

Birch has two types of dormant buds: short and long shoot. Short shoot buds are born on spur shoots that grow little under normal circumstances. They can replace the long shoot buds if these buds are destroyed. Short shoot buds produce the first mature leaves in spring and have usually completed growth by the start of summer. The terminal bud and several other buds near the terminal are long shoot buds; the shoots produced by these buds continue to grow and produce leaves well into the summer. The outgrowth from the long shoot buds is responsible for increases in tree height and crown diameter.

## Flowers

Birch trees produce flowers and seeds almost every year. The relatively long, thin structures of male flower buds are easily identified in winter when the leaves are off, as they are not hidden in buds, but exposed, usually at the ends of fine branches. There are often a pair of male flower buds forming a Y at branch tips. Female flowers are hidden in dormant buds and usually appear in early to mid-May, when male buds elongate and distribute their pollen. Many people are allergic to birch pollen and know almost immediately when the pollen starts to fly!

Birch seeds produced in the female flowers mature in late July and August. Seed dispersal usually begins in September and is mostly completed by November or December.

## Leaves

Leaves are the manufacturing centers of the birch tree; they are where carbon dioxide, water, and the sun's energy combine through chlorophyll to create the base molecules and energy necessary to meet the needs of the tree and the organisms that use birch as a source of food. This process, photosynthesis, is truly the greatest of natural alchemies.

The structure of the transportation system in the leaves—the venation—is a true work of art. These highways for water, nutrients and products manufactured in the leaves are often revealed by the activity of insects—referred to as skeletonizers.

## Sap

Sap streams through the sapwood, carrying nutrients and water, along with small amounts of sugar, to the leaves.

Birch sap is always compared to maple sap; there are several differences. The sugars in birch sap are the simple sugars, glucose and fructose, while the sugar in maple sap is sucrose (the same stuff in your sugar bowl). The birch sugars melt at a lower temperature and often caramelize, giving birch syrup a darker color and a taste more similar to molasses than maple syrup. The sugar concentration in birch sap is about one-half that of maple sap (about 1% versus 2+%).

*below left*
Mid-May female (top) and male (bottom) birch flowers in a usual arrangement.

*below right*
This photo shows what the female flower becomes—a mature birch catkin.

*far below*
An intricate network of birch leaves and fine branches.

*left*
Birch leaves chemically treated to show the leaves' transport systems.

*above*
April harvest of birch sap in northern Minnesota.

## Roots

Roots "explore" the soil, gathering water and the mineral and organic materials that are basic ingredients for photosynthesis. Roots also anchor the tree in the soil and come in a variety of sizes—from tiny ephemeral roots to the large woody roots at the base of the tree that grade into the main birch trunk.

## Fungi

Fungi associated with birch perform a spectrum of functions, both helpful and harmful. Some fungi help to gather water and nutrients essential for tree health and growth; others directly or indirectly result in loss of vigor and tree death.

## BIRCH'S USE AND CONTRIBUTIONS

Now that we understand how the tree and its different parts work, let's look at how the birch contributes to both man and nature.

### Bark

Birch bark is used in various ways by craftspeople and artists. The outer and inner barks are most often used, though harvesting second-growth bark and bark from dead trees is also common.

#### Outer bark

Outer birch bark was—and remains—important in creating two-dimensional art. Small sheets of bark are frequently used in place of paper and canvas as a medium for painting. Birch bark "bitings" (a traditional craft form) also utilize small sheets of bark; the folded bark is bitten with the teeth to make indentations in the bark that show the pattern. Collages use pieces of bark from living and dead trees of different sizes and shapes; bark from dead trees can be particularly important, as its color is often more varied than that of bark from living trees.

Throughout birch's range in North America, native peoples use sheets of bark in their basketry. The sheets are shaped by folding, then strengthened and reinforced with stem material from willow, hazel, and other species, and are finally laced together with materials such as spruce and willow root, as well as cedar and basswood inner bark. The most renowned of these "baskets" is the birch bark canoe, although baskets of all sizes and shapes are made for use in gathering, preparing, cooking, storing, and transporting food. These baskets are of great utility but are also fine works of art. Many works of present-day artists and craftspeople build on these age-old traditions as they adapt the uses of roots, summer and winter bark, and other plant materials to their vision.

Birch bark weaving seems to be the predominant use of outer bark in northern Europe and northern Asia (Siberia). Birch bark weaving has also been one of the main class themes at North House Folk School during its first decade. These classes are

Butterfly basket.
Mona Abdel-Rahman,
Minnesota, 2003.

rooted in the traditions brought to North America by Finnish, Swedish, Russian, and other immigrants from northern areas where white-barked birch species flourish.

Birch bark can also be valuable in areas outside arts and crafts. We cannot leave a consideration of the outer bark without mentioning its seemingly "magical" resistance to decay. Anyone who has hiked in a birch forest is familiar with the intact bark stovepipes from which the wood has been eaten by fungi and other soil organisms.

This resistance was recognized as a means of being able to store food, and led to the creation of birch bark containers—which some have called the original Tupperware. Modern science has identified many interesting chemicals in the bark of the birch tree, and laboratory tests have shown that these chemicals are the reason for its fungal decay resistance. Scientists at the Natural Resources Research Institute are working to develop medical, agricultural, and other industrial uses for these chemicals.

## Inner bark

The inner bark constitutes 75 percent or more of the bark layer. Although functionally it is critical to the tree—remember, the innermost layer is the transportation route for the distribution of materials manufactured in the leaves—it is not used as often commercially or in crafts as the showy outer layer is.

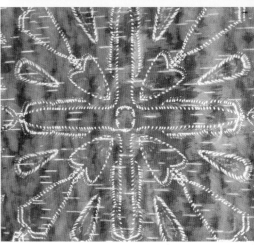

*elow*
*rch bark canoe. Eric Mase,*
*innesota, 2006.*

*ght top*
*heets of outer bark,*
*howcasing a variety of*
*xtures on the inner surfaces.*

*ght bottom*
*rch bark bitings are created*
*y literally biting a pattern*
*to a thin layer of outer bark.*

153

The chemical composition of the inner bark is different from that of the outer bark; the fungicidal properties of the inner bark are not as strong as those of the outer bark. However, books written on the use of native plants suggest that birch's inner bark has various medicinal uses. Remember also that ground-up inner bark was mixed with flour to increase the quantity of bread that could be made during periods of food shortage.

## Dead bark

Bark from dead trees can be used in a number of different ways: pieces of dead bark are used as a surface for painting, and "stovepipes" are often used intact as planters and to make birdhouses and the like.

The texture and color of bark from trees in various stages of decomposition can be very different from that of living trees. Dead bark tends to have much more color variety—from deep browns to almost black and lighter colors as well. The texture also seems to be a bit rougher and more porous than that of living trees. One of the most interesting ways of taking advantage of these texture and color differences is in creating collages.

## Second-growth bark

Birch basket. Ferdy Good, Wisconsin, 1996. The front panel is decorated traditionally with porcupine quills.

Second-growth bark, the inner bark that becomes the outer bark when the original outer bark is removed, is stiffer and generally more brittle than original outer bark. It is used as a sheet, not cut into strips or woven. Second-growth bark is used to make containers of various sizes and shapes; most often, these objects are made up of sewn-together panels that do not require a lot of folding and bending.

## Wood

Though we've spent a good deal of time discussing birch's bark, there is more to the birch tree than the bark itself. Among artists and craftspeople, birch wood is also desirable. It is often placed into two broad categories—normal wood and character wood. The distinction between green and dried wood is also important to crafters.

### Normal wood

Normal wood, in comparison to character wood, has greater strength and no defects; it is often used in making skis, snowshoes, toboggans, bowls, flooring, and paneling. The grain patterns of normal wood are straighter and, in some ways, less interesting.

### Character wood

In the past, character wood was considered unusable and was often relegated to the firewood pile or left in the woods to decay. Sources of character wood include layered burls, eye burls, spalted wood (black-lined wood resulting from fungal activity), "crotch" wood from major forks in the tree, spoon and coat-hook wood from branches, and other pieces of solid wood that have special shapes or coloration. These character woods are now sought after to create bowls, spoons, knife handles, and other specialty items.

*left top*
Bark taken from a dead birch tree.

*left bottom*
Assorted carved birch spoons. Fred Livesay, Minnesota, 2005.

*above*
Birch bowls. Erv Berglund, Minnesota, contemporary.

## Green wood

An extremely important distinction in working with wood is the difference between green, or freshly cut, wood and dry wood. Green wood is much easier to carve, and for carvers using only hand tools, green birch wood is essential. Woodturners also often rough out a bowl from green wood and finish after it has dried. In both hand carving and woodturning, the heartwood is often removed at the green stage; this reduces or eliminates the checking and cracking that often occurs as wood dries.

## *Branches and twigs*

Twigs and branches of all sizes are used for a variety of decorative and functional purposes. Small- to medium-sized twigs are often used to make decorative wreathes and to accent floral arrangements; small bunches of branches can be used to make sturdy and functional brooms; twigs are also harvested in early summer with leaves attached and dried for later use in the sauna where, when rewet, they provide a pleasing aroma.

Rope can be made from long, thin birch branches. This is done by twisting the branch, beginning at the thinnest end, and wrapping it around one's hand. The twisting and wrapping procedure bends or breaks the wood fibers, making the branch very supple. The branches can be used with bark on or debarked. Rope made in this manner makes a strong lashing material.

*right*
Root-burl-handled knives, John Beltman, Minnesota, 2005.

*far right*
Raven's-eye guitar. David Seaton, Minnesota, 2005.

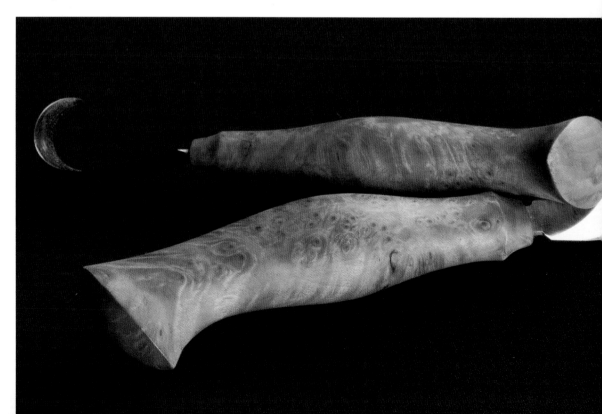

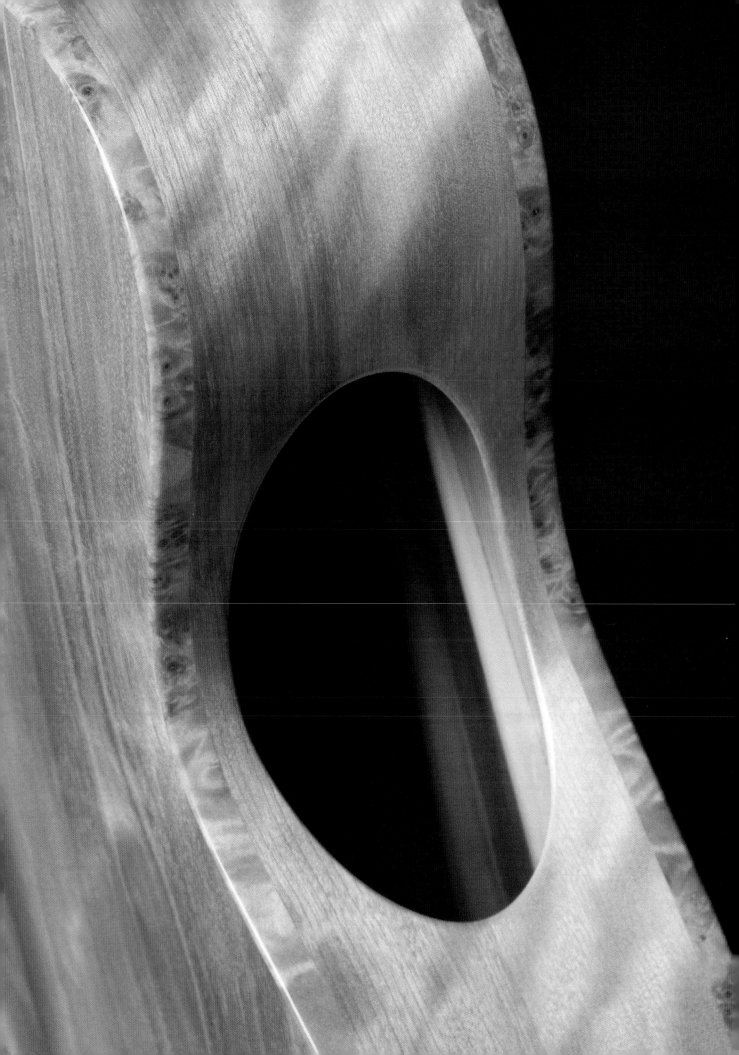

Medium to larger branches have many uses, depending on their size, amount of white bark, and degree of natural curvature. Branches with adequate size and natural curvature are used to carve spoons (see page 92). Forked branches are used to make hooks (see page 106), hangers, and shelf-supports. Larger branches and parts of the main tree trunk with significant amounts of white bark are used in the construction of rustic furniture—from picture frames to chairs and beds.

## Leaves

Leaves can be used to make medicinal teas and various extracts used in soaps and cosmetics.

## Sap

In late April and early May, before the leaves appear, sap can be harvested by drilling a small hole and catching the sap as it runs from the tree. Gathering birch sap is very similar to gathering maple sap and the methods used are the same.

Birch sap has been harvested for centuries in parts of the white birch world. Millions of gallons are gathered in Russia, Siberia, Korea, and Finland. Mostly, the sap is bottled and sold as a "natural" drink believed to provide mineral nutrients. Little birch syrup is made commercially in the United States; the main areas of activity are Alaska and parts of Canada. However, a few individuals in northern Minnesota have been known to gather sap, freeze it, and use it throughout the year as natural and healthy diet supplement.

## Roots

In northern Scandinavia, a beautiful and intricate basketry tradition is based on the birch root. Root extracts can also be used medicinally.

## Fungi

The early stage of wood decay caused by fungi, characterized by black swirling in the wood, is known as spalting. Spalted wood is frequently used in making birch bowls.

Fungi also has important medicinal uses. The conks, mushrooms, and other manifestations of these fungi have been harvested for centuries and used as food and medicine. A medicinal tea, common in Russia, can be made with several benefits, including treatment for some heart conditions and high blood pressure.

## Environmental Contributions

Besides having many craft-related, medicinal, and functional
applications in the human world, the birch tree also plays an
important function in the ecosystem by helping to ensure
productivity and sustainability of wood and other harvestable
plant materials. Birch trees also serve purposes unrelated to their
immediate economic value: they provide habitat for all levels
of plant and animal life; they play a part in nutrient availability
and cycling; they prevent erosion and maintain soil stability;
and they serve as "nurse" plants for other species, such as pines.
Additionally, birch trees provide the aesthetic qualities that we
value in our forests. When considering how to manage birch, we
need to consider long- and short-term economic factors together
with environmental and ecological factors.

## HARVESTING BIRCH

Now that we've reviewed the uses of the different parts of the birch tree, we'll discuss how to responsibly harvest birch. Following are some important points to remember when you decide to harvest birch:

- If you have no experience harvesting birch, ask an experienced harvester to assist you or harvest the birch for you. These procedures should not be undertaken by amateurs.
- Removing birch bark is a delicate procedure. If bark is removed properly from healthy birch trees, it will not kill the tree. However, removing bark improperly could kill the tree.
- Consult this book and other sources to learn proper harvesting times. Removing the bark, for example, most certainly affects the tree and changes the way the tree grows. The time of harvest denoted as "1" in the table is that time when harvest of bark is least likely to affect the tree.
- Try to remove bark from live trees in areas where they are likely to be cut in forest management operations, land clearing, etc. or remove bark from dead trees at the appropriate time.
- When harvesting birch bark, know who owns the land on which you are harvesting and get permission before harvesting. You may also want to have a project idea in mind before you go hunting for birch bark, but that is not a necessity.

### Times to Harvest

An integral part of understanding the uses of the various parts of these trees is knowing when they can be collected. Time of collection relates to ease of gathering, minimizing harm to the tree, and obtaining materials with the most desirable properties for a given use or project. The most commonly harvested part of the birch is its wood, mostly harvested for use in the forest industry. Generally speaking, little attention is paid to the time of year

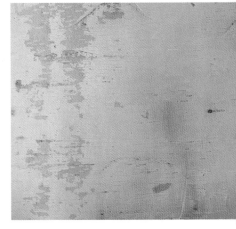

*above*
Inner surface of outer bark showing both winter (darker areas) and summer bark.

*below*
Birch bark basket.
Unknown, Maine, 2002.

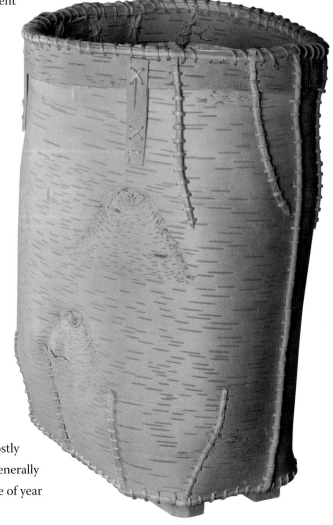

that wood is harvested for industrial use. For all other parts of the tree, however, there is a "prime time" for harvest. This time is determined by the growth of the tree, the effects of local weather on growth, and most importantly, the quality of the plant material that is harvested in relation to the needs of the user. The table below provides a general outline for harvest times. We'll look at timing and phenology in more detail as we look at the specific parts of the tree.

## Phenology of Gathering Paper Birch Materials

1—period of most activity (best time to harvest)
2—less activity but possible to harvest
3—least activity

| | APR.* | MAY | JUNE | JULY | AUG. | SEPT. | OCT. | NOV. | DEC. | JAN. | FEB. | MAR. |
|---|---|---|---|---|---|---|---|---|---|---|---|---|
| **Sap** | 1 | 1 | | | | | | | | | | |
| **Summer outer bark** | | 2 | 1 | 1 | 2 | | | | | | | |
| **Winter outer bark** | 3 | 1 | | | | 1 | 2 | 3 | 3 | 3 | 3 | 3 |
| **Inner bark** | | 2 | 1 | 1 | 2 | | | | | | | |
| **Leaves** | | 2 | 1 | 1 | 2 | 2 | | | | | | |
| **Branches** | 1 | | | | | | 1 | 1 | 1 | 1 | 1 | 1 |
| **Roots** | | 2 | 1 | 1 | 1 | 2 | 2 | | | | | |
| **Seeds** | | | | 3 | 2/3 | 1 | 1 | 2 | 3 | 3 | 3 | |

*April begins the growing season for birch.

## *What to Look For in Birch Bark*

Many people gather the bark first and figure out how to use it later on. It is useful, however, to know what "hints" the external features of the bark might give about the quality of the outer bark before it is removed from the tree.

The most noticeable feature is the diameter of the tree. The formula for the circumference of a circle is $2\pi r$ or $\pi d$; if you don't carry a calculator with you when harvesting, multiplying the diameter of the tree by three will give you a quick estimate of the width of the piece of bark. For example, an 8-inch-diameter tree will yield a piece of bark that is a bit over 24 inches wide.

There are a number of other features to consider, and most of them are easiest to discuss in terms of what to avoid.

**Thick, nonflexible bark** will not work for projects where strength and bark folding are involved. The bark you want to harvest for these kinds of projects should be flexible, which means you should be able to fold the bark on itself without cracking or breaking it. Tree size is a characteristic of maturity, and the bark of immature trees will almost always be thinner than that of mature trees. The bark from immature trees is often too thin for most projects; however, this bark can be used and does tend to be more flexible on average than bark from larger mature trees.

**Delamination** refers to how readily the annual layers of the outer bark separate; in some cases, they come apart almost as easily as pages in a book, which is desirable for projects requiring the bark to be split into layers. The bark should also separate easily from the tree.

A small test cut can be made low on the tree to loosen a small flap of bark to check for these characteristics.

**Rough bark** is usually found at the base of the tree. For this reason, bark is often removed from the trunk starting three or four feet above the ground. Serious bark gatherers might want to carry a ladder to remove long sheets of bark from even farther up the trunk.

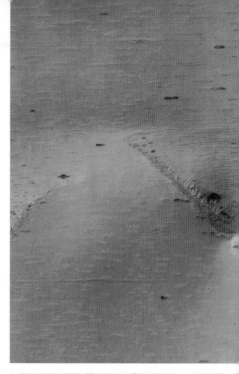

*below*
Outer surface of birch outer bark showing branch scar.

*right top*
Inner surface of outer bark showing branch scar.

*right bottom*
Outer surface of outer bark. The small lenticels in this bark are very desirable and make for better-quality bark than large lenticels. Note also the small branch scars.

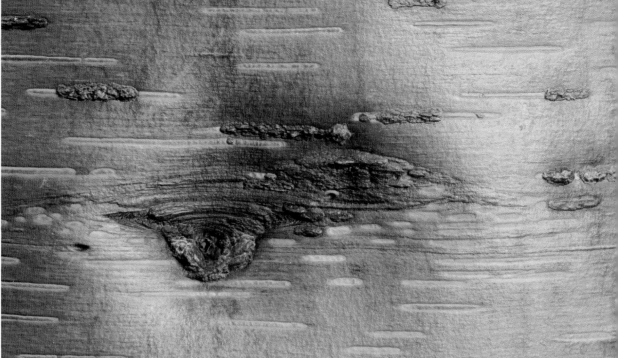

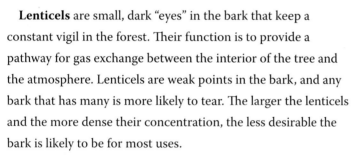

**Lenticels** are small, dark "eyes" in the bark that keep a constant vigil in the forest. Their function is to provide a pathway for gas exchange between the interior of the tree and the atmosphere. Lenticels are weak points in the bark, and any bark that has many is more likely to tear. The larger the lenticels and the more dense their concentration, the less desirable the bark is likely to be for most uses.

**Branch scars** are larger rough areas in the bark. Their presence almost always means that the innermost layer of the outer bark will have rough areas that may be hard to work.

Scars of various kinds indicate past damage from such things as pecking by birds or damage caused by falling trees and will almost always translate into roughness throughout the bark layers.

**Varying colors** are often found in the bark of immature trees. The color fluctuates greatly up to the time that the earliest bark begins to peel—when the tree attains a diameter of two to three inches. Colors vary from dark gray to diverse shades of rust. This color deviation does not impact the harvesting and can be useful if your project lends itself to several shades.

Although the above irregularities might make the bark less desirable for some uses, they also add character that can be interesting to incorporate into some projects. In other words, you needn't always avoid using bark with these characteristics. Instead, follow the above hints to gain interesting and useful information about the tree and a mental image of what the inside of the outer bark might look like.

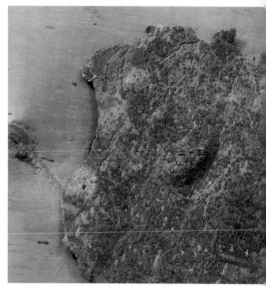

*far above*
Inner surface of outer bark showing small branch scars and lenticels.

*above*
The inner layer of the original bark is to the left; the bark to the right is the inner layer of second growth bark.

## Harvesting the outer bark

Bark can be harvested from living trees before or after they are cut. Tree anatomy and a general knowledge of the timing of tree growth are important for bark removal.

### Summer bark

Bark gathered from mid-June to early July is referred to as summer bark, and is lighter in color than winter bark. This is the time of year when it is easiest to harvest bark; luckily, this is also when the tree is least likely to be damaged by bark harvesting. However, it is important to remember that this time range can vary considerably from year to year, at different geographic locations in the same year, and among trees in the same stand. The dates given here tend to be averages based on the collective experience of several harvesters. Julie Kean, North House instructor and master basket weaver, uses the flowering of the wild rose as a signal that bark is ready to harvest. A sure way to determine the best time is to test trees periodically beginning in late May. This test usually consists of making a small cut in the tree near its base to determine how loose the bark is—this little flap of bark can also be used to determine other bark characteristics as well, such as the ones listed on page 162.

When the bark is really ready to be harvested, the outer bark separates from the inner bark with an audible "pop." Before the cut is made, the bark is under tension because the bark has not stretched or grown enough to adjust to the internal expansion of the wood. Both the cambium and the cork cambium are active, and these layers are fragile and easily broken.

*below*
John Zasada demonstrating how to roll freshly harvested bark.

*far below left*
John removing the bark from a birch tree.

*far below right*
Sheet of bark showing both summer (light) and winter (dark) bark.

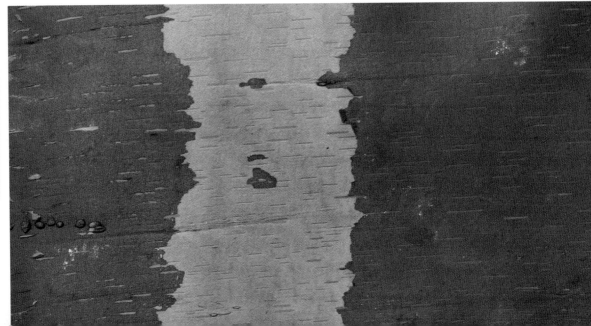

A shallow cut, usually less than one-quarter of an inch through the outer bark, is all that is required to remove the outer layer. When harvesting, try to do as little damage as possible to the inner layer of bark, and definitely avoid cutting through the inner bark to the wood. An easy way to regulate the depth of the cut is to use a utility knife that can be set for different blade depths.

Bark can be removed from the tree with just one vertical cut; this is the most common way to remove bark. The size of the sheets is determined by the diameter of the tree and the length of bark removed.

The bark can also be removed from the standing tree in a narrow strip two to three inches wide. This is accomplished by removing the bark in a spiral. This method is especially good when trees are relatively small in diameter. It is possible to remove a strip that is ten feet long, or more, from a tree that is six to eight inches in diameter.

Cut-down trees yield several other bark removal options, including the removal of all of the bark and leaving the cylinder of the bark intact. Canoe builders will take long sheets of bark from the entire branchless trunk with the hope of getting material large enough to make a canoe from the bark of a single tree.

Cylinders of bark can be removed from a short section of log when the bark is really loose. The time that this is possible is very limited, likely only a few days; both the cambium and cork cambium layers must be at their most fragile so that the wood and then the inner bark can be removed, leaving the intact cylinder of outer bark. The tree also needs to be fully hydrated so that there is enough water to keep these growth layers wet. The wood is removed from the bark layer (instead of the other way around) by using a knife or putty knife to loosen the inner bark layer and pushing or pounding with a hammer or mallet. This gives an intact tube of bark that can be used to make seamless containers; such vessels are fairly common in Russia.

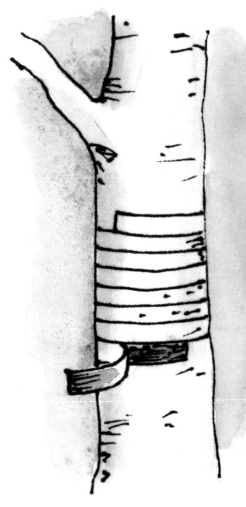

Bark can be removed in one long strip. This is a good technique for small-diameter trees.

## Winter bark

Winter bark is harvested when the tree's cambium and cork cambium are not in their most active period of growth. During this time, the cork cambium is not fully active and the inner and outer barks are still fairly well connected, making it much more difficult to separate the bark from the tree. Although some winter bark may be harvested in the winter season, bark with winter bark characteristics and colors is more likely to be harvested in

May, before the leaves are fully developed, and in late summer or early autumn, when leaves begin to senesce and fall.

At any other time during winter, it is possible to remove winter bark by bringing a frozen tree section into a warm and wet place such as a sauna or tub of hot water. When it warms up, the connection between the inner and outer bark may become softer and allow the separation of these two layers. Then, make a vertical cut and use a putty knife or tool of like width to gently pry the bark from the trunk.

So why go to all that trouble? Why not wait and harvest summer bark? The answer lies in the bark's color. Winter bark has a deep brown color, while summer bark is lighter. (Actually, when the bark is harvested just before the peak of summer bark harvest, the bark sheet may contain portions of both colors.) So for those with the patience and skill, the extra time spent harvesting winter bark is rewarded with a beautiful piece of bark that has a rich brown inner layer. This winter bark is often etched and scratched with animal figures or geometric designs to give special character and significance to canoes or baskets.

Etched basket. Eric Mase, Minnesota, 2006.

## Bark from dead birch trees

As trees lose vigor, their growth rate slows to almost nothing. The outer bark on trees with many dead branches does not become as loose as in healthy trees during the prime harvest time and is difficult to separate from the inner bark. Dead or unhealthy trees do not expand as much as a healthy tree, and the fragile layer that develops between the inner and outer bark does not develop as it does in healthy trees. The inner bark can be removed with a knife or file, but it is best to find a tree where the separation has occurred naturally; this bark has better color and texture than bark that has to be physically separated. Once a tree is dead, it often remains standing for a number of years. During this time, the bark layer separates from the wood, and eventually, the inner bark begins to decompose. When this happens, the outer bark can be removed more easily, although there are often pieces of inner bark attached. Once the tree topples, decomposition of the wood occurs more quickly. Stovepipes require practically no labor to harvest; the decomposition-resistant outer bark layer remains after fungi and bacteria have removed or loosened the wood and inner bark.

Stack of flat sheets and rolled bundles of birch bark.

## Second-growth bark

As mentioned earlier, removing the outer bark does not typically kill the tree, but it does greatly change the appearance of the tree. If bark removal is done correctly with minimal damage to the inner bark, a new layer of outer bark will develop as a result of the inner bark and cambium's activity. The second-growth bark that appears after the outer bark has been removed is utilized and harvested differently than original outer bark, and is vastly different from the previous bark layer in appearance and texture.

Once the outer bark is removed, the outer layer of the inner bark dries and changes color. For example, when summer bark is removed, the inner bark will change to a deep brown color by the end of the summer. During the next growing season, this new outer bark turns black and begins to crack into rectangular pieces of varying sizes and shapes. Over a period of years, these individual pieces fall off, creating an array of colors and textures on the under layer.

Birch bark harvesters from Sweden note that the second bark will be thick enough for a project and ready to harvest about 20 to 25 years after the first bark is removed.

## *Transporting, Storing, and Preparing Bark*

There are two things to consider after the outer bark is harvested: getting the bark out of the woods and storing it after it leaves the woods. Once the bark is off the tree, it can be transported from the woods in flat sheets or in rolled-up bundles. If in rolled-up bundles, the bark should be rolled with the outside in and "up or down" the tree, not rolled the way that it was on the tree.

Birch bark can be stored for many years in flat sheets or rolled bundles if kept dry and out of the sun, but soaking or heating may be necessary before beginning a project with stored bark, though preparation depends on the individual bark and how it will be used. A sheet of bark is more likely to require this treatment than bark that will be used in strips for weaving. Rolls of bark can be difficult to unroll if the bark is very brittle; it is often advisable to soak a roll of bark before attempting to unroll and flatten it.

For use in basketry, birch bark stored for a year or more may have to be soaked or heated to bring back softness and flexibility. A combination of heat and moisture is more effective for softening bark than unheated water alone.

*far above*
Original bark (white) and bark that replaced original bark after it is removed (dark).

*above*
These birch stars demonstrate the variety of colors available from dead tree bark.

A good way to create these conditions is by using a sauna; you can also steam bark by holding it over a kettle of boiling water. Personally, I prefer putting bundles of bark in a plastic bag with several cups of water and heating them in my sauna for a day at 160 to 190 degrees; this procedure softens them nicely. For small unsoaked pieces or strips of bark, heating for 15 to 20 seconds in a microwave oven is a quick solution.

Bark may require cleaning, splitting, or other treatments to make it ready for use. Splitting bark is a technique used to create thinner, more flexible layers or to remove undesirable parts of the bark. The ease of splitting varies greatly among birch trees—some bark can be split into layers almost as easily as turning pages in a book; other bark seems almost impossible to split. Splitting around some of the rough places in the bark adds an additional challenge.

One common problem when splitting is that one side of the split tends to get thicker than the other. To remedy this, the thicker side should be pulled on harder—this will make the two halves of the split more equal.

## HER CURRENT CONDITION

A major part of harvesting birch responsibly is understanding its current condition and what we can do to ensure the future of birch. A process called forest inventory is updated annually to assess the condition of the forests across the United States. This inventory tells us such things as the acres of birch forest, the age structure of the forest, tree size, and other interesting facts that give a pretty good picture of birch's condition.

In a nutshell, the inventory tells us that most of the birch is mature to overmature and that there is little birch being regenerated as existing birches die or are harvested. To put this in perspective, consider the aspen, a major associate of birch. Aspen readily regenerates: as it is harvested, new aspen forests spring from the earth. Because of its ability to sprout from its roots, each aspen tree can produce as many as 50 to 100 new trees when harvested. Birch does not have this regenerative capacity. The birch is replaced by several sprouts originating from buds at its base—and there is less than one birch tree regenerated for every tree that dies or is cut.

In our forests today, we see many birch skeletons and dying trees. The reasons for natural mortality are largely related to the fact that much of the birch is overmature and very susceptible

to stress brought on by drought and other adverse weather. These stresses reduce tree vigor and greatly reduce their ability to survive attacks by insects and fungal pathogens. These stresses often act in concert—for example, a series of dry years will increase the susceptibility of the tree to insect invasion that it could resist in years with normal rainfall.

## HER FUTURE

Birch has served humans well over the centuries. It is up to each of us to be concerned about the fate of our birch forests—or all forests, for that matter. Questions often heard today among those who craft with birch are: Is the way that we manage and use birch presently sustainable into the future? Can we be assured that the birch will always be a part of the forest and available for the many uses described in this book? It is difficult to project the future, but there are some current developments and issues that are important to consider that directly and indirectly relate to what the future holds for the birch tree.

The issue of global climate change is very real; with a warming climate, birch will move north and become less common in the lower 48 United States than it has been in the past few hundred years. Climate warming, rain and snowfall changes, storm intensity, and increases in carbon dioxide, ozone, and other atmospheric gases will affect growth, regeneration, and the way birch responds to stress from native and introduced insects and diseases.

A completely different consideration is the industry that is developing based on the commercial extraction and use of the chemicals in the birch bark. Several companies have developed methods to extract and purify these chemical compounds, which have been shown to have a variety of potential uses, including medicines, lubricants, and seed coatings that protect agricultural crops. If some of this potential is realized, it will revolutionize both the way birch is used and its economic value.

The fate of birch forests is in the hands of landowners and forest managers. Many unique and innovative uses of the tree have been described in this book, but almost all harvested birch is used in the forest industry. The majority of that use requires the tree to be chipped into little pieces and reconstructed as paper or various types of particleboard and chipboard. Certainly, some birch is used for lumber and veneer, but the fate of most trees is to be turned into chips and reconstituted by various industrial processes.

Those of us who use birch bark or other unique parts of the tree often shed a tear when we see a load of logs heading for the mill. We know that we could have used the bark or a crook in the tree to create a unique bowl or basket.

Although it is impossible to use every scrap of bark or unique piece of wood, it is possible to have better coordination between the forest industry and birch crafters. An important step toward this partnership is recognizing all of the things that can be made from the birch tree as it grows. The flow chart on page 171 helps to illustrate various raw materials that come from the tree during its life cycle—some require harvesting the entire tree, others only parts of the tree.

There are a number of ways to coordinate these different uses of the tree. The most common method currently is for an individual needing bark or other materials to contact the landowner. The landowner gives permission and may charge a fee for the right to harvest. Permission to harvest should take some of the following factors into consideration—access to land, necessity to harvest at specific times of the year depending on the material being harvested, and opportunity to obtain materials before the trees are harvested should there be a plan to cut the forest for industrial use of the wood.

Besides the coordination mentioned above, there are opportunities to harvest materials from areas where no large scale tree removal is planned. The ethics and concerns involved here are two main ones—obtaining permission and knowing how to harvest bark, branches or other materials in a manner that does minimal damage to the tree.

The future of birch is in question for a variety of reasons—some over which we have direct control and others over which we have none. Birch is a very resilient species, but the current philosophy of forest management of birch has been "Let nature take its course"; this strategy will not maintain birch in all areas and on all types of sites where it is desired. Current harvesting targets healthy and dying forest areas. Although forest management strategies include working in stands of all ages, the main need now is to assure adequate birch regeneration. Relying on natural processes to reforest birch may provide acceptable results in some areas, but in others there is a need to utilize common regeneration practices used for other tree species, such as manipulation of the forest floor and surface soil to provide desirable seedbed conditions;

Open lines of communication between crafters and the owners of soon-to-be-harvested birch stands could preserve otherwise wasted bark for use in projects.

artificial seeding and planting of birch where seeds are not available; and protection from browsing during early growth when seedlings can die from over browsing.

What are the factors that will determine the presence and availability of birch, and how do we best utilize what is available? There are no absolute answers to these questions. They require some thought by all who use and appreciate birch, if it is to be an important part of the future forest.

Birch must remain a part of these forests. These trees are an important part of our forests, and to many, they define the North Woods. Even outside the North Woods, people from all walks of life find spiritual value in what author and artist John Peyton has called the "bright tree of life and legend." The reasons are economic, ecological, and spiritual and are considered throughout this book.

And we do know how to encourage birch regeneration and health; we know practices such as forest thinning will maintain the health of birch. They should be used when needed to ensure a birch presence. For the sake of the tree and future human generations, we should give the dear birch the help it needs.

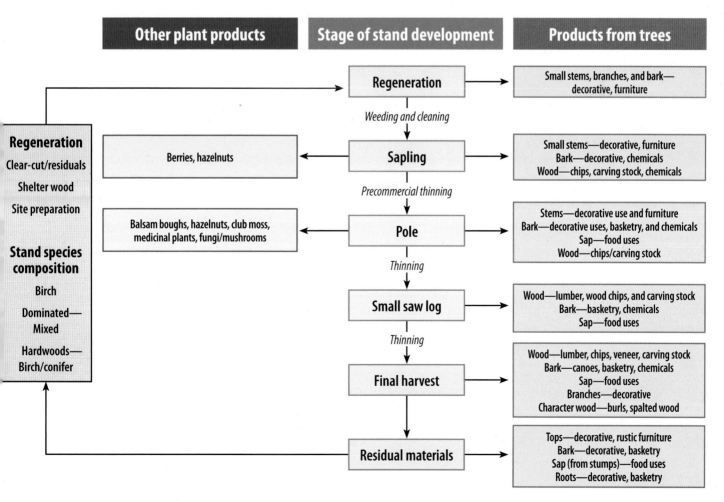

171

# CONTRIBUTORS

### ROGER ABRAHAMSON
*How-to Craft Artist*
Roger is a traditional bowl turner. Using a spring pole lathe, hand-forged tools, and freshly harvested native woods, he specializes in the creation of Norwegian ale vessels. His fascination for these objects has its roots in his immigrant grandmother's ale bowl, which is still in the family. He has been a turner for eighteen years, working with a pole lathe exclusively for the past twelve.

### BETSY BOWEN
*Illustrations, Design, Editorial Team*
Betsy spends her days happily making woodblock prints and writing and illustrating children's books. Her social life is based around North House committee meetings. She lives on an old homestead near Grand Marais with her photographer/geographer husband.

### PHILIP BOWEN
*Principal Photographer*
Philip began his photographic work as a youth, with black-and-white film and a darkroom in the pantry of his family's farmhouse. He now shoots sports events in North America and Europe, when he is not coaching or playing Ultimate Frisbee or cross-country ski racing. Phil and his wife recently moved to Uganda.

### MARK HANSEN
*Contributing Craft Artist*
Mark has a particular interest in workboats of the North and has studied boat building in Greenland and in Norway. He has built birch bark canoes, Greenland kayaks, Umiaks, Norse prams, and a variety of traditional wooden sail and rowboats of the North. His other interests include winter camping with a traditional outfit, wooden skis, and birch toboggans. Actively involved in the founding of North House Folk School, Mark has been teaching since 1995 and operates Hansen Boat Works.

## JOANNE HART
*Contributing Poet*

Joanne has made her home on the Grand Portage Reservation since 1972, and she writes poetry to acknowledge the respect for life she is so often taught to recognize there. Joanne has been writing poetry since she was a child. Her craft is currently fostered by the place at Pigeon River where she lives gratefully with the isolation of wilderness and the support of the community of Grand Portage Anishnabeg. She has eight grown children who continue to inspire her life.

## JULIE KEAN
*Contributing Craft Artist*

Julie has been making baskets and ornaments since 1981. She utilizes materials gathered from the woods around her home in Hovland, Minnesota. Her favorite materials are birch bark and red osier dogwood. In 2001, her artistic talents were featured on the program *Venture North* on public television. At times, Julie integrates other natural materials into her work, including pinecones, driftwood, and spruce roots.

## LAYNE KENNEDY
*Contributing Photographer*

An editorial photographer, Layne shoots feature assignments for a variety of magazines worldwide. His two most recent books focus on the Minnesotan region: *Jewels on the Water—Lake Superior's Apostle Islands* and *Minnesota—Yesterday and Today*. He is currently working on two new book projects, *Invisible Landscapes from the Edges of America* and a book on Iceland. Layne conducts two seasonal photography workshops at the North House Folk School.

## FRED LIVESAY
*Contributing Craft Artist*

Fred discovered his woodworking skills at age 10. He later trained as a wheelwright and carriage builder for seven summers and then went on to study Scandinavian folk art, decorative arts, art history, and museum studies. Fred is currently a museum consultant but still finds time to build and repair fine furniture, carve spoons, turn bowls, weave baskets, and do handiwork of all kinds. Fred has taught at North House Folk School since its beginning and also instructed at the American Swedish Institute.

## LISE LUNGE-LARSEN

*Contributing Writer*

Lise, a native of Norway, is a professional storyteller and award-winning children's book author. When she's not traveling to tell stories or busy writing, she can be found at her home in Duluth, Minnesota, working on her garden, biking or hiking in summer, and cross-country skiing in winter. Birch is her favorite tree.

## CHARLIE MAYO

*Contributing Craft Artist*

Since the 1970s, Charlie has had a consuming interest in birch bark. He has traveled to Scandinavia many times to study with the masters while pursuing this interest. He has demonstrated at Rice Lake Audubon, the American Swedish Institute, Luther College, Norsk Høstfest, and the Minnesota State Fair. Charlie is a founding board member of North House Folk School.

## KURT MEAD

*Contributing Craft Artist*

Author of the award-winning field guide *Dragonflies of the North Woods*, Kurt is a passionate dragonfly enthusiast who has given dragonfly presentations and workshops across Minnesota and traveled as far as Sweden (the birthplace of Kubb) to pursue his love of dragonflies. He has biology and art degrees from the University of Minnesota at Duluth and was drawn north by love and to work as a naturalist at Wolf Ridge Environmental Learning Center. He is now a stay-at-home dad, an author, a homesteader, and a part-time naturalist and has hopes of never working a full-time job again. Kurt makes Kubb sets from birch harvested sustainably from his homestead and is also North House Folk School's Kubb expert. He claims to be the Roadkill King of Finland, Minnesota.

## SCOTT POLLOCK

*Design, Celebrating Birch Exhibit Curator*

"Building the bridge between tradition and an aspiring set of human hands" best describes Scott's interest and investment at the North House Folk School. Scott spends his workday visiting with a group of devoted educators to develop programs for North House. When not crafting it out on the keyboard, he can be found keeping the lights on in the woodshop carving toys, boats, and skis—all benefits of having time off to spend with his two young boys, scraping out a playful existence in the North Woods.

### ANNE PRINSEN

*Manuscript, Design, Editorial Team*

Anne grew up around birch trees. When she was little, she began thinking of stories during car trips out West to avoid her pesky older brother. Her passions still lie with words, trips, and thoughtful design.

### HARLEY REFSAL

*Manuscript, Editorial Team, Contributing Craft Artist*

Harley is an internationally recognized folk artist who specializes in Scandinavian-style flat-plane figure carving, a minimalist style that leaves the tool marks exposed. He has won numerous carving awards and has taught carving classes throughout the United States, Canada, and Scandinavia. In 1996, he was decorated by the government and King of Norway for his contributions to Norwegian folk art studies. He is the author of *Art and Technique of Scandinavian-Style Woodcarving*. In addition to his carving and teaching, Harley is a professor of Norwegian language and Scandinavian folk art at Luther College, Decorah, Iowa. He has also served on the North House Folk School Board.

### MIKE SCHELMESKE

*Contributing Craft Artist*

Mike's interest in Native American and Scandinavian traditions has kept him constantly pursuing boreal forest crafts and materials for project ideas. He particularly finds utility craft intriguing, and the thought of putting his crafts to work on an everyday level keeps him searching for the next project. Whether it's carving toys from basswood blanks for his daughter, Aurora, or shaping canoe paddles from a crooked knife he fashioned from an old file, Mike's ingenuity and his approach to craft are refreshing.

### LARRY SCHMITT

*Contributing Craft Artist*

Recently, Larry has become interested in radical natural dyes—the exploration of the discovery of natural dye processes. Larry teaches nålbinding, weaving, and other fiber arts courses at North House Folk School. He came to the fiber arts by learning nålbinding from his parents. Larry has been involved in teaching and researching nålbinding for more than twenty-five years. The instructional manuals he has written on the subject are some of the only resources on nålbinding in English.

### JON STROM
*Contributing Craft Artist*
Look for the wood chips flying and you're sure to find Jon. Jon is a sculptor, woodworker, and log builder with a strong interest in Swedish spoon- and bowl-carving techniques as well as the history of log building. He has demonstrated at Grand Portage National Monument, Old Fort William, and White Oak Society and has taught at various workshops.

### DEBORAH SUSSEX
*Principal Photographer*
As a photographer and outdoor educator, Deborah has traveled extensively both in the United States and abroad while on assignment for numerous national publications. An avid Nordic skier, cyclist, and back-country camper, she lives with her husband in Ely, Minnesota and owns a successful gallery and portrait studio.

### GREG WRIGHT
*North House Folk School Executive Director*
Chasing horizons in the North has been a preoccupation of Greg's for many years now. An avid wilderness traveler by water, ski, and foot, Greg has journeyed across much of northern North America, exploring the traditional waterways of the Canadian Shield in wood-canvas canoes, encountering elemental landscapes and echoes of Arctic cultures while paddling Arctic rivers in the barren lands, and engaging the North's defining season of white on skis and snowshoes at every opportunity. Greg became North House's Executive Director in 2001, bringing with him numerous years of experience in his craft, educational, and nonprofit leadership. Greg, his wife, and their daughter live just outside of Grand Marais, Minnesota, on their homestead with organic gardens, beehives, a wood-fired timbered sauna, and a view of the northern horizon.

### JOHN ZASADA
*Manuscript, Editorial Team, Contributing Craft Artist, Celebrating Birch Exhibit Curator*
The biology, ecology, use, and management of birch in northern forests has been a favorite topic of John's for many years. He is a recently retired research forester and has worked with birch in Alaska, Wisconsin, and Minnesota. He began taking classes at North House with Charlie Mayo and has continued to try to understand the growth and use of birch and other tree barks; he also enjoys experimenting with birch bark weaving.

# ACKNOWLEDGEMENTS

Just as North House Folk School emerged and continues to exist today thanks to the collective efforts of many inspired individuals, *Celebrating Birch* is indebted to the talents, dreams, efforts, and determination of many. The book's striking visual images, artfully crafted projects, and multidimensional text and stories all exist thanks to the community of instructors, contributors, writers, editors, and photographers who agreed to engage the project. Their creative efforts speak for themselves.

*Celebrating Birch* found its inspiration in part from the Celebrating Birch exhibit, first shown in 2004. Curated by John Zasada, the exhibit emerged in 2004 at the MacRostie Gallery in Grand Rapids, Minnesota; in 2005 at the Jacques Art Center in Aitkin, Minnesota; and in 2006, co-curated by Scott Pollock, at the Johnson Heritage Post gallery in Grand Marais, Minnesota. Many thanks to these three supportive organizations for making the exhibit possible.

North House Folk School appreciates the ongoing support and involvement of many institutions. In particular, North House wishes to thank the City of Grand Marais, the Grand Portage Band of Minnesota Chippewa, Grand Portage National Monument and Minnesota Wood Campaign.

Numerous other individuals helped nurture and support the project at many different stages. Thanks to Staci Drouillard, David Prinsen, Carol Harris, Jacquelyn Tofte, Steve Downing, Emilie Zasada, Julie Miedtke, and untold others who recognized the value of this project from its inception.

Finally, North House Folk School thanks its many friends, partners, supporters, volunteers, instructors, students, staff, interns, and advocates. Together, we have given shape to a dream that enriches the lives of people every day. May the work of our hands, our hearts, and our minds continue to affirm the shared journey ahead.

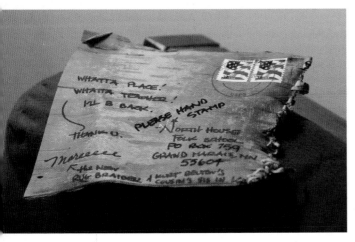

Birch bark postcard.

## CELEBRATING BIRCH— THE GIVING TREE EXHIBIT

In 2006, North House Folk School invited a number of instructors, students, and friends to be a part of an exhibition to celebrate the elemental beauty of craft. The exhibit featured the birch tree and its uses through more than 300 contemporary and historical objects created by over 50 artists and craftspeople from five different countries. North House partnered with the Johnson Heritage Post Art Gallery of Grand Marais, Minnesota, to host the exhibit. The following photos in this book are taken from the Celebrating Birch—The Giving Tree exhibit: endpapers, v, ix (left), 1, 2, 3, 4 (above bottom), 5 (above), 5 (right), 8 (left), 15, 48 (below), 48 (right), 54 (right), 63, 66, 67, 72, 74, 75, 76, 77, 78, 80, 81, 82, 84 (above), 84 (below), 85 (above), 85 (left), 86 (right), 87 (left), 87 (right), 87 (above), 89 (above left), 89 (above right), 90, 100 (below), 101, 110, 114, 122 (right), 146 (left), 147 (left), 152, 153 (below), 154, 155 (left bottom), 155 (above), 156 (right), 156 (far right), 160 (below), 166 (above).

## PHOTO CREDITS

**Betsy Bowen:**
172 (middle), 173 (top)

**Philip Bowen:**
front cover (second to left), front cover (right), v, vii (right middle), xi (below), xi (right top), xii (top), xii (bottom), 10, 11, 12, 13, 16, 17, 18 (right), 19, 20, 21, 22 (right), 23, 24, 25, 26, 27, 28, 29, 30 (right), 31, 32, 33, 34, 35, 36, 37, 38, 39, 40 (right) , 41, 42, 43, 44, 45, 46, 47, 49, 50, 51, 52, 53, 55, 56, 57, 58, 59, 60, 61, 62 (right), 64, 65, 68, 69, 70, 71, 93, 94, 95, 96, 97, 98, 99, 100 (right), 102, 103, 104, 105, 106 (right), 107, 108, 109, 111, 112, 113, 115, 116, 117, 118, 119, 120, 121, 122 (bottom left), 123, 124, 125, 126, 127, 129, 130, 131, 132, 133, 135, 136, 137, 138, 139 (top left), 139 (top right), 153 (right top), 154 (right top), 158, 160 (top), 166 (below), 172 (top), 172 (bottom), 173 (second from top), 173 (second from bottom), 174 (all), 176 (bottom), 177, back cover (flap), back cover (second from left), back cover (second from right)

**Rick Brooker:**
164 (below), 164 (far below left)

**Stephan Hoglund:**
174 (bottom)

**Layne Kennedy:**
front cover (below), ii, vi, 4 (above top), 7, 140, 147 (top), 172 (second from top), 173 (middle)

**North House Folk School:**
xi (right bottom), 6, 18 (left), 22 (left), 30 (left), 40 (left), 54 (left), 62 (left), 106 (left), 174 (second from bottom)

**Jay Steinke:**
xiv

**Deborah Sussex:**
front cover (left), front cover (second to right), front cover (flap), endpapers, vii (right bottom), ix (left), ix (right), 2, 3, 4 (above bottom), 5 (above), 5 (right), 8, 15, 48, 54 (right), 63, 66, 67, 72, 74, 75, 76, 77, 78, 80 (left), 80 (right), 83, 85, 86 (right), 86 (left), 87 (above), 87 (right), 88, 89, 90, 100 (left), 101, 110, 114 (right), 122 (right), 146 (left), 146 (below right), 152 (above), 153 (below), 154 (below left), 154 (below right), 155, 156, 157, 160 (below), 166 (above), 176 (top), back cover (left), back cover (right)

**John Zasada:**
150 (below left), 150 (below right), 151 (above), 151 (left), 153 (right bottom), 162, 163, 167

**Other:**
173 (bottom) provided by Lise Lunge-Larsen, 176 (middle) provided by Greg Wright

**Stock:**
1, 79, 149, 150 (far below), 168 (both), 170

## ILLUSTRATION CREDITS

**Betsy Bowen:**
36 (left), 128, 139 (bottom), 142, 143 (left to right), 144, 145 (left to right), 148, 165

**Fred Livesay:**
114 (left)

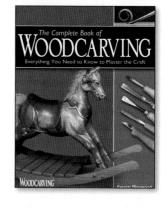
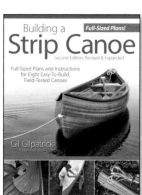
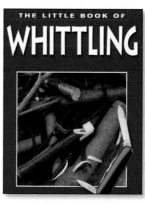

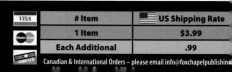